A Gift of Love

A Gift of Love

Gail Magruder

OLIPHANTS

OLIPHANTS
MARSHALL, MORGAN & SCOTT
A member of the Pentos group
1 Bath Street
LONDON EC1V 9QA

Copyright © 1976 by Gail Magruder and Laura Hobe

Originally published in the United States of America by
A. J. Holman Company, a division of J. B. Lippincott Company

First published in Great Britain 1976

ISBN 0 551 00764 8

In order to help preserve the privacy and well-
being of persons mentioned in this book, the
names of some individuals have been changed.

Printed in Great Britain by
Hollen Street Press, Slough
677082L30

Dedicated in love to all those who had the courage
to love us when we needed it so desperately.
Thank you, Lord, for the visible signs
of your love for us:
 the letters
 the gifts
 the hugs
 the tears
 the prayers—of your people.

With thanks and love to Laura Hobe, without whose help I never could have completed this book.

Prologue

I REMEMBER THE FIRST TIME I went water-skiing. It was a beautiful day, with a bright sun that made the air sparkle. My father was driving the power boat and my sister Ruth was along. When my mother was very young, she had been the first woman in the Los Angeles area to water-ski, and naturally my sister and I were expected to follow her example. Ruth, who was a few years older than I, had already begun and now it was my turn.

When I looked over the side of the boat into the choppy water, the sun no longer felt warm on my back. The water looked cold. It was very deep out there, and although I was a good swimmer for my age, the thought of getting out of the boat frightened me. I didn't want to do it. Yet when my father said, "Gail, get into the water," I couldn't refuse. My fear would have disappointed him. My father could do so many things very well that he assumed his daughters were equally gifted. He expected us—the first time out—to get into the water, put on our skis, and not fall off. And that is exactly what I did. I was afraid not to.

1

FROM THE VERY BEGINNING, I didn't want to move to Washington. We were happy where we were. I had grown up in Los Angeles, so I was comfortable there. Jeb and I had a house we loved. It was near the ocean, which we enjoyed. We had friends. Jeb had a small business that was just beginning to be successful enough for us to live comfortably. We had four healthy, beautiful children—Whitney, who was nine, Justin, seven, Tracy, five, and Stuart, two. Whitney and Justin were in school, and I didn't want to take them out in the middle of a semester and move them across the country to a totally different environment.

Besides, I didn't like politics. Perhaps that isn't a fair way to put it. Like Jeb, I had been a political science major in college, and I *did* like politics. It was the politicians I didn't like. I had known them on almost every level, from the bottom on up, and it seemed to me that they ran too fast. They were willing to give up too much for the prizes they sought.

Jeb was more tolerant, perhaps because he not only liked, but loved, politics. If he could have made his living at it, he would have done it fulltime. But he couldn't support his family by running campaigns, so he did his political work on the side. That was another reason why I didn't like politics—it kept Jeb away from me and our children.

But this time, it wasn't the Don Rumsfeld campaign back in Chicago, where Jeb had begun his political career in 1962, three years after we were married. Nor was it the 1968 victory of Richard Nixon, which Jeb had helped to accomplish by managing a successful campaign in Southern California. The invitation to move and to go into politics fulltime came from the White House.

We had moved several times during the ten years of our marriage, and politics had been one of the reasons. In 1966, when Jeb gave up a promising job with the Jewel Tea Company in Chicago, he was trying to repair some damage to our marriage. Between going to school at night and becoming involved in politics, he was hardly ever home, and the strain was beginning to show on all of us. As long as we lived in Chicago, it was almost impossible for Jeb to reduce his political work load because he had been so successful. To him, the only solution was to move and not get involved in politics again, so when the Broadway-Hale Company in Los Angeles offered him an attractive job, he took it. He made his decision a little too quickly. The job he accepted was new and not as clearly defined as he expected, something a good administrator should have avoided. And Jeb was a *very* good administrator, which eventually became apparent to some of the politicians in Southern California. Soon after we moved to Los Angeles, and in spite of his best intentions, Jeb got caught up in politics again.

I didn't like the fact that my husband had said yes to Bob Haldeman's offer before he could even talk it over with me and the children. But I could understand why he did it: he was only thirty-five, and it wasn't every day a man that young was offered a position as Special Assistant to the President. I didn't really expect him to say, "That sounds pretty good to me, Bob, but let me find out how my wife feels about it." Nevertheless, I wish there had been some way for him to do that.

I was uncomfortable about going into a new and unknown environment. I had done it before, but each time it became more difficult to say good-bye to friends and familiar surroundings. Washington was completely different from anything we had ever known.

I didn't like the fact that, by accepting his new position, Jeb would be taking a $10,000 cut in salary. He was making that much more from his own business, which he now would have to sell. I had lived in the East for a short time when I was in college, and I knew it would cost more to live there than it did in Los Angeles. Washington living, I had heard, was astronomical. My apprehension was hardly eased when Jeb told me that Bob Haldeman said Jeb would have to find the means to get himself and his family to Washington. Moving expenses weren't in the White House budget! I couldn't believe it: we had to sell our house, move our belongings across 3,000 miles, buy a new house, sell our two old cars (which never would have made it to the East Coast), and buy two other cars when we arrived; Jeb's plane fare would be reimbursed, but not mine or our children's. Moving would cost us about five thousand dollars. Any corporation would have paid those expenses.

My biggest objection was the fact that Jeb was to go to Washington immediately, which meant that the children and I had to stay behind to sell the house and prepare to move. I didn't know it then, but that was going to take two months.

I could have objected more strenuously, I know that now. But one of the reasons why hindsight is always clearer (and not very realistic) is that it forgets a lot of the pressures that make us behave the way we do. At the time, I couldn't have handled the guilt I would have felt if I had become an obstacle in the way of my husband's happiness. And he was happier than I had ever imagined he could be.

A lot has been said about—or against—Jeb's ambition. He had a healthy amount of it, which was always considered a plus for him in every other job he had. But he also loved to work and was very good at it. The invitation to the White House meant that his work had been noticed and appreciated. He would also have an opportunity to affect our country's future. In the face of that, I stifled my objections.

Still, I had a foreboding of unpleasant things to come. I

kept it to myself because I wanted Jeb to know he could count on my support. Also, it would be hard enough on our children to be uprooted again without having a reluctant mother in the bargain. So, just as we had done several times before, we all began to look forward to a new way of life.

We sold our house immediately, but finding one in Washington took quite a bit of looking. Packing alone took a month, and I never could have managed it without Jeb if it hadn't been for the Morelands. Mrs. Moreland, a wonderful woman, was our babysitter. She and her husband came over every evening and helped us pack our dishes and books and all the other things that suddenly became very dear to us in their familiarity. They were with us the day before we moved, and I remember how we stood in a circle, holding hands, while the Morelands prayed for Jeb, the children, and me to be happy in our new home. The Morelands often prayed aloud, and while I wasn't comfortable doing so myself, it felt good having someone do it for me.

Our house was filled with people on moving day. Friends and neighbors came to say good-bye. Before we left for the airport I looked for my engagement ring and couldn't find it. I assumed I probably had packed it in my suitcase which was already on its way. The children and I went through the empty rooms quickly, saying good-bye to the house we had loved so much. Our footsteps sounded loud and hollow.

It wasn't until we got to Washington that I had time to unpack my jewelry box. When I opened it, I saw that I had been robbed. Someone with a selective eye had taken whatever was valuable and left the costume jewelry. Unfortunately, I hadn't realized that when people move there are always a lot of strangers coming and going in the house. Among the missing pieces were a ruby and gold ring my father had had made for me when I was sixteen, and my diamond engagement ring.

2

WASHINGTON IS A DAZZLING CITY. To live there as a member of the White House Staff is like experiencing weightlessness: one simply floats unobstructed. Except that the floating is done at 90 miles an hour!

There were those little conveniences that spell luxury. If we wanted a table at Sans Souci, we simply had the White House switchboard make the reservation. We were often able to use the White House boxes at the three theaters at the Kennedy Center for concerts or plays. If we had to go to the airport, a limousine picked us up at our door. Someone was always on hand to take care of our luggage. Occasionally, when Jeb had to work at Nixon's Western White House (San Clemente), he was able to take me and the children with him. We went on one of the Air Force courier planes, which were far more comfortable and spacious than any commercial flight. Inside they were divided into compartments, and passengers were seated according to their importance. Usually we were considered important enough to sit in the forward compartment, where there were roomy swivel chairs. We were served excellent food and our choice of drinks. In case we wanted to call anybody—anywhere—there were phones available.

Arrival at El Toro Air Force Base, near Camp Pendleton, California, was a pageant. The plane was met by limousines bearing the proper seal and flag, which allowed us to be waved right past all the guards, each of them saluting as we passed. I remembered how different it was when I was in college and had a boyfriend who was at El Toro. He invited me out to the base once in a while and I was stopped at every checkpoint and asked to produce identification. But I was just plain Miss Civilian then. Now red tape simply did not exist.

We had a pleasant house in Bethesda. It wasn't as large as we felt we needed, but it was the best we could afford, given the real estate values around Washington. Eventually we would find something larger—but that could wait. We weren't spending much time in our home anyway.

The pace of life threatened to overwhelm us from the moment we arrived. Our names were automatically put in the Green Book, the directory of "important" government and business leaders, which meant that we were on the "official" party list—and Washington is a partying town. We had invitations from lobbyists, socialites, embassies, businessmen, congressional members, and people who just wanted to get together for a few drinks and do business in a relaxed, sociable atmosphere.

At first, my inclination was to back away from so many after-hours activities. But I soon realized that if I wanted to see my husband at all I had better join them rather than fight them. So, if I didn't want to be like most wives of White House Staff members—waving good-bye to my husband at 7 A.M. and not seeing him again until 11 at night, or later—I had to go along with him.

I'm not one of those mothers who finds the company of her children boring. I enjoy them and try to be with them as much as I can. But I found myself having to choose between them and my husband when it came to evening hours and weekends. It was a difficult decision to make, but I made it in favor of Jeb. The long hours he worked eventually would strain his relationship with the children and me. If I holed up at home, soon there might not be any relationship at all. But if I went with him to as many functions as I could squeeze in, I might at least be some sort of a bridge between him and the children.

Thank heavens for Alicia! Looking back, I think that whatever stability our home had during those first few years came from her. She is a warm, loving woman from El Salvador who had seven children of her own back home, yet she mothered us all. She lived in with us, which gave me the freedom I needed to be with Jeb. Our children adored Alicia, and that made me feel less guilty for all the times I had to leave them in her care. Sometimes we were out five nights in a row, occasionally at parties, but more often at "working dinners" or official events such as the opening of a new play at Ford's Theater.

At first the parties were exciting. Almost everyone I met had a name I recognized from the newspapers, and there was a sense of being at the very core of the world's most important events and decisions. The embassy parties were fascinating. Inside those marvelous old buildings were beautiful art exhibits, which gave us insight into the lives of the people in the countries they represented. It was fun, too, to become acquainted with the traditions of other cultures. One of the highlights each spring was the birthday of Queen Elizabeth, whose health was toasted with strawberries and champagne in the garden of the British Embassy.

Washington also is a city of charity benefits and special performances by some of the world's outstanding artists. We were frequently invited to them. Like the parties, they were lavishly arranged, with excellent food and far too much to drink. Only recently I heard that Washington has one of the highest rates of alcoholism in the country, and I find that easy to believe.

By the time we began to make the rounds of parties during our second year in Washington, we became aware of things we hadn't noticed before. The glitter was wearing thin, and we could see what lay beneath the surface. Not every face was new to us. We recognized many of the people we met and we began to realize not so much who was who as who was with whom. And the who wasn't always with the proper whom. In fact, quite often this was the case. Wives lost out to secretaries and "friends" to a degree that made us uncomfortable, especially when we knew the wives.

Jeb and I were either too young or too old to fit in with most of the other White House Staff members and their families. The top-echelon executives were older than we were and their children were almost grown, so there was little reason for us to meet except at special White House functions. I admired Jo Haldeman, Jean Erlichman, and Patti Colson—but from a distance. They had a certain composure and an inner beauty I found attractive, and the few times we met I was impressed by their warmth and thoughtfulness.

Most of the White House Staff members were younger than we were and had small babies, so it was difficult for them to get out together. They had very little money to spend on babysitters and had to pass up many of the invitations they received. I was sorry for the wives. Without exception they were bright, well-educated, attractive—and lonely. While they spent all day and most of the long evening hours at home with their babies, their husbands were having a glorious ball flying back and forth between California and Washington, or to anywhere else they found a reason to go. I say, "found a reason" because it seemed to me, standing as I was on the outside, that many of their trips were unnecessary. But almost anyone would find it hard to resist the thrill of summoning a plane and being able to tell the pilot where he wanted to go —in style.

The White House Staff also had its jet-setters. They were young men—mostly in their late twenties or early thirties— who were independently wealthy and had bought their government positions. Their jobs weren't important, but they enjoyed the prestige of their association with the President's staff. They and their wives could afford to live it up—and they did. At parties, they were the ones who arrived earliest, drank the most, and left last. Being in their company was a sad, disturbing experience. They laughed compulsively and kissed and hugged each other as if they were desperate for a good time. Some of them were on their way to becoming alcoholics, and there were rumors of wife-swapping. The wives were beautiful and well-dressed, yet they too were often left at home while their husbands went off for days or weeks at a time. Surely these young women must have wondered why they couldn't go along on some of the trips, especially when so many secretaries did.

I was lucky in having a husband who wanted to be with his family and didn't like to travel. He went where he had to go, but whenever possible he took me and one or two of the children with him. I don't think I could have coped with the situation if he hadn't.

Undeniably Washington offered advantages for our children. Our oldest boy, Whitney, was accepted at St. Albans when we applied in 1972, and, while there are those who might say it was because his father was Deputy Director of the Committee to Reelect the President, we prefer to believe it was because our son is a very bright boy. A few years later, when Jeb was an embarrassment rather than an attraction, Whit was still at St. Albans—and a leader in his class; and, more significant, Justin was accepted during the heat of our crisis.

We lived in a neighborhood where there were many children, and new friendships soon began to replace those our children had to leave behind. The warmth and friendliness of many of our neighbors were blessings to Jeb and me. The quiet wisdom of the Millers, a retired couple next door, and the immediate acceptance as part of "the family" by the

Gillespies, life-long Washingtonians, who lived across the street, made our transition easier.

Our children were old enough to be interested in the city, and some of my most pleasant memories are those of our visits to Washington's excellent museums. The Smithsonian was a favorite that lured us back time after time. Occasionally, we even got Jeb to come along with us to an art museum, although he did it to humor me. He seemed too preoccupied, too much in a hurry to lose himself in the contemplation of a painting—looking back on it convinces me that everyone needs to make time for the calming influence of art in his life. Something purely creative and timeless has to balance the insistent immediacy of our existence.

We enjoyed bringing the children into the White House and showing them the areas tourists never see. It was fun to see their excitement when our car drove past the saluting guards at the White House gate. They were proud of their father. But they also missed him. The White House soon became "Daddy's office" where Daddy was spending long days that extended into night. Its glitter was a poor substitute for the Saturdays and Sundays when we all used to drive to the beach in California and have a family picnic.

From the very beginning, Jeb must have sensed what was coming, because as soon as we arrived in Washington he bought us bikes and had a bike rack fastened to the back of his car. He was determined to spend every moment he could with us, although later I learned that he took a lot of teasing for it. Almost every Saturday, unless the weather got in our way, Whitney, Justin, Tracy, Stuart, and I piled the bikes into our car and drove down to the White House where Jeb usually worked until 12 or 1 o'clock. A sign on our visor—"EAST EXECUTIVE DRIVE, PARKING SPACE No. 16"—got us past the guards into the parking lot at the White House. We parked our car, waited until Jeb joined us, then unloaded the bikes. Stuart used to ride in a seat on the back of Jeb's bike.

The picnic hamper was fastened to the back of mine. Whitney, Justin, and Tracy had their own bikes. And off we'd go —around the Ellipse, to the Lincoln Memorial, the Washington Monument, and along the beautiful Potomac paths. It wasn't the ocean, but we loved it every bit as much because we were together. Once the pressures were all behind us "back at the office," Jeb became another person, one we dearly loved and yearned to have with us more of the time. He truly relaxed and played with the children until all of us became silly with laughter. When we got hungry, we pulled off under some trees and opened our picnic basket. These were the times when we talked most easily with each other.

That is—if the pageboy didn't buzz.

The pageboy was a black plastic receiver about the size of a pack of cigarettes which Jeb carried with him at all times. It enabled the White House to contact him wherever he was within a fifty-mile radius. It buzzed—not too loudly, but noticeably—and after the sound of the buzz the signal corpsman in the White House communications office would ask Jeb to call either the White House or some other number.

Most members of the White House Staff were obliged to carry a pageboy because theoretically they were on duty twenty-four hours a day. At night the "beeper" lay on our bedside table, which was hardly necessary because in our home, we also had a special telephone with a direct line to the White House. If anyone wanted Jeb during the night, which was often, he used the phone, not the pageboy—unless our phone was already busy, and often it was. Sometimes at night, when I couldn't sleep, I used to lie there in the darkness watching the lighted telephone button that told me Jeb was talking to someone, and I wondered how so many things could possibly be so urgent that.they couldn't wait until morning.

Our Saturday picnics were often interrupted by the pageboy. By then, we were trained to notice the location of telephone booths as we rode along, and Jeb would go to the nearest one. Sometimes it was important—the President had ordered American troops to invade Cambodia and a statement had to be prepared to counter the negative press reactions. But more often it was someone on *Air Force 1*—or some other courier plane—who felt almighty powerful telephoning someone on the ground from up in the sky—about something that could have waited until he came back home.

I realized that this was no ordinary job my husband had. He was working near the nerve center of the most vital office in the world, dealing with problems that affected the lives of millions of people not only here but in other countries. I didn't expect such an office to operate on a strict nine-to-five schedule. We live in an explosive world where events have no regard for individual timetables. I could accept the fact of the pageboy because there were times when Jeb had to be reached in a hurry. What I couldn't accept was the casual way in which it was used, almost as if it were a toy in the hands of children.

I had expected the White House to be demanding, but I was not prepared for its possessiveness. At times it seemed to me that Jeb was not supposed to have a life outside its walls. When we went beyond the fifty-mile radius, we had to notify the White House switchboard of our whereabouts. Once, after Jeb had spoken at Williams College, his alma mater, we left Williamstown and drove through the Berkshires to the Albany airport. No sooner had we entered the terminal than we heard, "Mr. Jeb Magruder! Mr. Jeb Magruder!" over the loudspeaker. The voice was anxious and Jeb raced to a phone booth. There was a message. The White House switchboard had succeeded once again in tracking us down during the brief five minutes we were in the airport.

We weren't the only ones. From my conversations with the wives of other staff members, the routine was the same for everyone. Men left home early and returned late. A child, especially one who had to be tucked in early, saw very little of his father. Most of the wives seemed resigned to accept this way of life, yet there was a pathos about their loneliness.

In a sense, although the name of Martha Mitchell has become the symbol of exaggeration, she was typical of the White House Staff wife. I know that she made life difficult for a lot of people, but somehow I can't be impatient with her. Neither can I dismiss her as a kook. It always seemed to me that her behavior was a cry for attention, a way of saying "Please notice me—I am a human being!" And, while the other staff wives may not have pleaded so obviously, they had every reason to feel the same way. One had only to go to a staff get-together to understand why.

Chauvinism is a word I never took seriously until I was in the company of White House Staff members and their wives. At the dinner table, the men talked among themselves; the subject matter was usually the same one that occupied them all day, all night and most weekends: politics and government. The women hardly talked at all—not that anybody told us we shouldn't talk, but nobody listened if we did. After dinner the men formed a tight little group of their own and the women were left to themselves. I found it interesting that these men had married women of intelligence, yet seldom seemed to credit them with any.

I was not a stranger to the business world. My husband had worked for several corporations and we had been to numerous corporate functions. While I can't say that women were always appreciated as persons, I have never seen them so excluded. It was as if we didn't exist.

Even among the women, White House politics was an all-consuming subject. If they enjoyed any of Washington's abundant cultural life, they seldom mentioned it. They didn't mention books or current events. Their conversation was about government and those who worked in it.

Perhaps Jeb and I had an advantage in having moved so often. We were accustomed to dealing with a new environment, to discovering the things of interest in it. Most of the other staff families had come to Washington directly from their hometowns and still felt like strangers. Yet they also behaved as if they would never have to leave.

Once I asked a few women what they and their husbands were planning to do in the future, after the President's second term in office. They looked at me as if I had said something shocking, and I gathered that such thoughts were kept hidden deep in their subconscious minds.

I was uncomfortable with the men on the White House Staff. I didn't like the feelings I had about them, and I realize now that my discomfort was a warning signal. Bob Haldeman appeared to be cold, brusque, unrelating, like someone from another planet. He had absolute tunnel vision that excluded everything but his objective. Yet his wife was so warm and delightful that I felt something about him must be nice for her to have married him. Chuck Colson just plain scared me because he was overwhelming. He spelled trouble. Bob Mardian was crude and his language coarse. And John Dean impressed me as a brilliant but slippery person I did not feel I could trust, although I didn't know why. I thought Larry Higby, Bob Haldeman's "gofer," was a friend, and I was wrong.

But I loved John Mitchell, or, rather, I loved what John Mitchell was to my husband. He treated Jeb like a son, as he did several other young men in government. In fact, I have often wondered whether this kindly, soft-spoken, thoughtful man has ever realized how many adopted sons he has. Jeb was devoted to him, and so was I. Only he seemed to realize that a man did not live by work alone. He seemed to be pleased when Jeb and I were able to have some time alone together.

I hated the kind of jokes I heard when the White House men got together. There was little humor in them. Almost without exception, they were dirty jokes or degrading attacks on specific individuals and groups. I couldn't laugh at things like that.

There were so many other things about the White House that seemed "unfortunate," as I chose to call them. I felt a mixture of fear and excitement when I went there to pick up Jeb on Saturdays or after work on our way out. I know that security precautions are necessary, but I didn't like the sight of so many guards. To know that there were men with rifles standing in glass enclosures on the roof of the Executive Office Building and the White House was frightening. Everywhere I went there were locked doors, passes to be shown, television monitors, and more guards. To me, it underlined the ever-present threat of violence that goes with twentieth-century life, especially at the sources of power. Jeb had even been reprimanded for the "unusual activity" in the East Executive Parking Lot that first Saturday we had gone biking —as if there had been something threatening about persons aged two, five, seven, and nine.

For an outsider, I saw quite a bit of the office.

Jeb and I had very little time together, and so we agreed to have dinner or lunch out at least once each week. In that way, we could be away from the telephone, which seldom stopped ringing. Usually I would meet him at his office near the end of his day—about 7:30 or 8 p.m.—and wait for him to finish work. I also used to pick him up when we were on our way to a party or some other function. For a few months before the 1972 election, I worked at the Committee to Re-elect the President (CRP) headquarters, writing background reports on the campaign issues in some of the states.

I didn't like many of the things I saw. Frequently, when I arrived to pick up Jeb, I had to wait as long as one or two hours before he was free, usually because at the very last minute he would be given something that "had to be done immediately." Why couldn't it have been given to him earlier? —or the next morning? Why couldn't they give some thought to these things? Or to the people involved? I was frustrated by the way human beings were treated like so many disposable objects.

At all three offices—the White House, the Executive Office Building, and the CRP headquarters across the street—I was disturbed by the familiarity of some secretaries and their bosses. I had heard the jokes about Washington secretaries, and I had to agree that there was some basis to them. In fact, I used to tease Jeb by asking, "How do they hire their secretaries? According to the color of their eyes and their measurements?" Sitting around Jeb's office for so many hours at the end of the day, I heard too many references to times they had spent with their bosses.

My husband is a handsome man, and I saw the way women looked at him. I can't say I was worried about that at the time, because I knew what Jeb and I had together. But I couldn't help wondering: would it ever happen to us in the years ahead? Did everyone in Washington *have* to be that way?

Jeb and I usually had been able to tell each other how we were feeling, so I didn't keep my doubts from him. He knew how I read some of the people around us, but he was a far more trusting person than I was and used to pooh-pooh a lot of my remarks. Sometimes when I complained about their jokes or their attitude toward women, I felt like a nagging wife—and I think Jeb thought I was. I was uneasy disliking these men who were so close to a President I admired and respected, and because my own feelings were so discomforting, I kept trying to forget them.

My only chance to talk with President and Mrs. Nixon came when we went through a White House receiving line. I was honored to be there at all, and when the President shook my hand and asked me something personal, such as "How is Whitney getting along at St. Albans?" I marveled at the way a man with so many critical issues on his mind could remember that we had a son, much less his name. Later—perhaps even months later—I learned that Steve Bull or one of the other young aides whose offices encircle the Oval Office had briefed the President just before the occasion: "Jeb Magruder is one of the guests, his wife's name is Gail, and their oldest child, Whitney, goes to St. Albans. . . ." I felt disappointed, yet at the same time I felt I had no right to be. A President is a busy person, perhaps the busiest in the world. Of course, he couldn't be expected to know all those details. Someone *had* to fill him in. He had more important matters on his mind. That's the way it is with busy people—*of course, it's all right!*

It wasn't the system that was wrong, I told myself. It was *me*.

3

FOR ME, WATERGATE BEGAN long before the actual break-in.
The facts were there for me to see; yet I didn't see them.

One day in January 1972, Jeb made a remark that left
me wondering if I had heard him correctly. It was a typical
husband-wife conversation about "What went on at the office
today, dear?"—although for us it was hardly typical, because
we rarely had time for such exchanges. Jeb was talking about
some far-out schemes to sabotage the campaigns of the
Democratic candidates for the Presidential nomination. He
told me about Gordon Liddy's suggestions, which included
such things as prostitutes, blackmail, and kidnaping.

I was sick with disgust. This is what men close to the
President spent their time talking about! I couldn't believe it!

My reaction startled Jeb. He was so caught up in Bob
Haldeman's mania to get information about everyone and
everything that I don't think he ever gave a thought to the
fact that such activities were illegal and unethical. I knew it
was standard procedure in political campaigns for each side
to spy on the other side, but this was evil. I felt as if I were
living a scene in a Fellini movie:

"What did you do at the office today, dear?"

"Oh—we talked about kidnapings, muggings, prostitu-
tion. Nothing special."

During most of Jeb's day, he didn't breathe the same air
I did. He lived in an atmosphere charged with the acrid odor

of suspicion, fear, and distrust, and it was harder for him to realize that the rest of the world was not that way—or that threatening. It was also the beginning of the campaign, and many people forget that in the early part of 1972, Senator Edmund Muskie was considered the man to beat in November. And that, most Republicans agreed, would not be easy. Bob Haldeman wanted to wage total war from the very beginning. And in war, you use some pretty nasty weapons. Just how nasty and where you drew the line was difficult, perhaps impossible, for Jeb to see at that point. He didn't have the time to think about such things—in fact, he didn't have time to think about anything.

Jeb began to work longer hours as the campaign got under way; we almost never had time to be alone together. When he was home the phone rang incessantly. Our life was more hectic than ever. The only time we really had a chance to talk was when we were alone in the car going to the airport or downtown. But that wasn't enough for us to give each other sufficient feedback.

And so, when Jeb saw how much he had shocked me with his remarks about campaign sabotage, he did the expedient thing: he tuned me out. The reason I remember the event so well is because from that day on, Jeb became more guarded about telling me what went on at the office.

He never was the same again. I was aware that he was preoccupied, but I blamed it on the campaign. The pressure was building up almost visibly week by week. I also knew that Jeb was beginning to look beyond the election, wondering what kind of a future he would have in government. He was hoping for an appointment to a job that required Senate approval—perhaps something like Director of Action, which included the Peace Corps and Vista. But he couldn't be sure whether he would be rewarded for his work on the campaign —or dumped. He understood the men he worked with well enough to realize that it could go either way.

I didn't like what was happening to us, but I didn't think

there was anything I could do about it. My concern for our children became even greater than my concern for Jeb. They hardly saw him anymore, and they needed him every bit as much as I did. I made it a point to spend as much time with them as I could, in the hope that more of my presence would compensate for the lack of Jeb's, but, of course, it didn't work. Children can't be fooled. They felt the same way I did—we all would be glad when the campaign was over and things were normal. How wonderful it would be to return to a life where Jeb was not so distracted and strained.

It was in June of 1972 that I began to fear that there wouldn't ever be any "normal" again. We were in California at the Beverly Hills Hotel when Gordon Liddy telephoned Jeb and told him that James McCord and others had been caught trying to break into the Democratic Campaign headquarters at the Watergate Hotel. It was a dizzying weekend of meetings with California Republican Party leaders and celebrity parties, and I was not aware of what was happening. Jeb succeeded in keeping it from me, which wasn't hard to do, considering all the commotion around us. I remember hearing the name "James McCord" and recognizing it as the name of the man in charge of security at CRP headquarters, nothing more.

Jeb had always been an outgoing, gregarious, relating person. Now he was becoming moody, introspective. I didn't know it then, but the extent of his involvement with something illegal was getting through to him. And at the very moment that he was beginning to face the truth about what he and the others had done, he was joining in their attempt to cover up their guilt with lies.

He was irritable with me and the children. I was miserable, but, more than my own pain, I felt the pain of our children, who couldn't understand why Daddy rebuffed them when they tried to jump on his lap or roughhouse with him. As he became more and more nervous, he complained about any noise they made. I tried to get through to him, but he put me off with excuses about the pressure of the campaign. By then, I knew it was something more. Jeb had always worked well under pressure—he was the kind of person who not only created it but could take it. Why, all of a sudden, when the campaign was going so well and the reelection of Richard Nixon seemed assured, was he cracking? I was beginning to gather up the pieces of the picture, but I was reluctant to put them together. I was afraid of what I might see.

Richard Nixon was reelected, and almost immediately we were caught up in plans for the Inauguration, which Jeb was appointed to manage. All of a sudden, everyone wanted us to get tickets to the Inaugural events. We were contacted by friends we hardly knew and relatives we had never neard of. At least, it took my mind off our personal problems—but not for long.

In June, August, and September 1972, Jeb was called to testify before a grand jury investigating CRP campaign practices. Two of those times he perjured himself.

Our relationship was so damaged by that time that we couldn't even discuss the accusations that were being made. Our communication was zero. I can't say that I suspected Jeb of being involved in anything illegal. I don't think I was able to face that possibility squarely. But certain things troubled me and made me doubt. Each time Jeb had to go before the Grand Jury, he had been extremely nervous, which wasn't like him. Speaking before a group of any size never had bothered Jeb before. Maybe he had a few butterflies inside himself, but to look at him, you would never know it. He was always Mr. Cool. Why was he so worried about appearing before twenty-seven men and women? On the nights before he had to testify he couldn't sleep. He kept getting up and going to the living room so he wouldn't keep me awake with his restlessness.

Yes, then I knew something was wrong. The jury believed Jeb, but that didn't make me feel any better. He was too defensive. He was taking tranquilizers and sleeping pills. He was drinking more and drinking faster. I couldn't believe that I was actually grateful he was seldom home with the children. I didn't want them to see him that way.

For the first and only time in our marriage I thought about divorce. I didn't exactly consider it, but I couldn't keep the prospect out of my mind. It was like having a back door there, a door I might someday have to use, because I knew I could not live much longer with a man who was as alienated as Jeb was.

The momentum of the Inauguration got us through the beginning of 1973. When it was over, it took Jeb a month to clean up all the details. Then he was offered a job with the Department of Commerce. He called it a "holding position," which meant that the job was created for him and was only temporary until a position requiring Senate confirmation could be arranged. Jeb took the job in March. To his surprise, he liked it very much.

So did I. And so did the children. For the first time since we had come to Washington four years earlier, Jeb was working a normal day, five days a week. We were beginning to have dinner together as a family. Only one thing didn't change. Jeb and I were strangers to each other. He was lost within himself somewhere and I didn't know how to reach him.

One month later James McCord began to tell the truth about the Watergate break-in. Jeb had been named by McCord as one of the conspirators. Three days after he sent a letter to Judge John Sirica, our home was invaded—by reporters and photographers from every newspaper, wire service, and television news program in town. They all wanted to talk to Jeb, to ask him how he could direct a campaign and not know what was going on in it. There were television news vans parked at the curb in front of our house—and in front of our neighbors'! Reporters and photographers stood in clusters at the end of the walk. Some came right up to our front door so that the moment anyone left the house he found a microphone thrust in his face.

Jeb didn't want to answer questions. He was going along as best he could with the cover-up story, realizing, of course, that it was coming apart. But the other members of the White House Staff didn't see it that way. As long as they couldn't agree on what to do, Jeb felt he could do nothing. He stopped leaving by the front door and went out by the backyard and over a neighbor's fence to the next street where he had begun parking his car. The reporters never caught him.

When they were unable to interview Jeb, the press became almost hysterically determined to get information—*any* information—from anyone who would answer a phone or come to a door. Some reporters telephoned our neighbors, not only at their homes but where they worked. They called us at all hours, from dawn to midnight, and sometimes in the early morning hours. We had an unlisted telephone number and changed it two times, but they always got it within a few days. Finally we stopped changing the number because the only people who couldn't keep up with it were our friends.

I felt that our home was being violated. The reporters and photographers seemed completely insensitive to the fact that we were human beings. Their aggressiveness frightened me. Jeb was more patient with them than I was. He kept saying they had a job to do. I realized that, too. I imagined how it must feel to be told to get the story—or else. I could tell from the way some of the reporters and photographers apologized to me when they called up or rang our doorbell— "I'm sorry to bother you at a time like this"—that they really didn't want to be doing what they were doing. It was fright-

B

eningly similar to the way the White House expected people to get the job done no matter how they felt about the way they had to do it. In both cases, the ends justified the means.

Nevertheless, I couldn't see how the press expected to learn the truth about Watergate by camping outside our home. Every morning they would arrive around 6 o'clock. They were in small or large groups, depending upon what kind of news was breaking, holding a cup of coffee in their hands, surging forward whenever anyone left the house, sometimes going around the back and looking through our kitchen windows.

Each day on their way to school, our children had to walk through the crowd at the end of the walk. Finally they began cutting across the grass to avoid them. And then, one morning, I knew how it felt to lose control of myself to the point where I could have killed.

Whitney was cutting across the lawn on his way to school when Leslie Stahl, of CBS-TV, suddenly rushed from across the street toward him. She was carrying a microphone and was followed by a cameraman who undoubtedly was ready to record her interview with our twelve-year-old son.

"You get away from my child!" I shouted. "If you have something to say, you come to me—but don't you *ever* come near my children!" I knew then that if Leslie Stahl had been standing near me I would have attacked her. Perhaps at that moment I was insane with fear—fear for my husband and children, fear of being considered less than human, fear of things I did not yet understand but sensed were evil, and fear of my own rage.

Luckily for us all, my behavior froze everyone where he stood. No one even took a picture. Not a word was spoken. Leslie Stahl retreated and Whitney went on his way. Our children were never approached again.

Finally I put the pieces together. My husband had been involved in illegal actions and would have to pay for what he had done.

At the beginning of April, the grand jury reconvened to look into new evidence concerning the Watergate break-in. This time Jeb would not lie. He had decided to go to the prosecutors and tell them about his involvement. He and I began to meet with his lawyers.

At that point, I couldn't even guess what was going to become of us. Not only was Jeb's future uncertain; I really didn't know what was going to happen between us. I had almost come to the decision that either he should move out or the children and I would. I was in agony for him, but he had cut himself off from me to such an extent that I couldn't be part of his pain or comfort him. When he decided to go to the prosecutors I stayed on, not wanting to add to his misery.

Tormenting as it was to face the possibility that Jeb might have to go to prison, something good also began to happen. As soon as he began meeting with his lawyers, Jeb's relief was visible. He wasn't torn between lies and the truth anymore. His loyalty wasn't stretched to the breaking point between his employers and his family.

The first day Jeb met with the prosecutors he was gone for a long time. When he came home, I was startled by the look on his face. He was tired, but he was smiling just a little. For the first time in months, he was relaxed. He didn't want a drink. He seemed so happy to see me. Although he would never be the same, he was recognizable as the man I had loved and married—and still loved very deeply. We put our arms around each other and stood there in the living room for a long time, holding each other close. I had my husband back, and at that moment it mattered more than anything else in the world.

4

JEB WAS TO WORK with the prosecutors for the next fourteen months, sometimes intensively day after day, sometimes for two or three days a week. The experience almost destroyed him.

He wanted to tell the truth. He admitted he had broken the law and was prepared to pay the penalty for it. But he thought he could tell his part of the story without involving anyone else. How mistaken he was! The prosecutors wanted to know everything. They wanted names, dates, background —who was there and who did what. It was especially painful for Jeb to implicate John Mitchell.

John Dean approached the prosecutors shortly before Jeb did, but he argued with them for weeks, trying to get total immunity. He didn't succeed, but he did obtain some conveniences which became obvious later. Jeb was the first to cooperate fully, without trying to bargain for immunity. He and John Dean were to become the key prosecution witnesses in the Watergate trial. Unfortunately for Jeb, John Dean has a computerlike mind which can recall the exact time of the exact day on which he ate blue cheese on rye bread. Jeb is just the opposite. He recalls the large picture, not the details. Very often it was difficult for him to remember dates and the sequence of events, and the prosecutors became impatient. Obviously they didn't believe he was telling the truth. Again and again they made him go over the story. At their interrogations, they encircled him, called him names, and swore at him. They wanted to break him down.

The prosecutors were young—in their late twenties and early thirties. Most of them knew their lawbooks but had had very little experience dealing with people. They didn't understand that Jeb was a trusting person. He wasn't a lawyer and didn't insist on all his rights because he really didn't know what they were.

The prosecutors also were working from the perspective of liberal Democrats. To them, Jeb was a Nixon Republican, which meant he was filth. They treated him accordingly. When he came home after spending a day in their office, he was so exhausted he practically crawled in on his hands and knees. The degradation of not being believed ate at his remaining self-respect until there was hardly anything left.

And during all this time there was a living to be made. Jeb had resigned from the Department of Commerce when he decided to go to the prosecutors. Another job was out of the question. Who was going to make an offer to a man who might be going to prison?

There were three or four businessmen who wanted Jeb to work for their companies on a consultation basis, so he set up his own business and took them on as clients. We thought of it as a temporary measure, something that might keep us going for a few months. We had no idea it would last over a year.

What made it particularly difficult for Jeb was the way the prosecutors kept calling him back for still another retelling of the campaign details. They didn't care whether he had an appointment with a client; they simply told him to be at their offices on such-and-such a day. Sometimes that happened several times a week.

In June 1973, when Jeb testified before the Senate Watergate Committee, the press returned to our neighborhood. Now they began to call our friends in cities where we had lived before—Kansas City, Chicago, Los Angeles—trying to find out something about our "past." They got to Jeb's mother and father in Santa Barbara. For several nights in a row when Jeb was away on business, Christopher Lyden of *The New York Times* woke the children and me by pounding on our front door at 11 o'clock at night. Each time I opened the door he insisted I tell him where Jeb was, and when I told him Jeb was away on business, he insisted again and again that he had "a right to know the truth." The last time I closed the door in his face I stood there shaking with rage. We had absolutely no control over our lives. We couldn't plan how we were going to survive—now, or while Jeb was in prison, or after he came out. We seemed to live each day at the mercy of people who were trying to manipulate us at the same time they were denouncing my husband as the manipulator of all time.

I hated having our children see pictures of their father on the front pages of the newspapers. It was not only humiliating, but dangerous. Our lawyers had suggested that we ask the children's school officials to be especially alert to strangers loitering around school grounds. We were celebrities now, they told us, and there was always the possibility of a kidnaping. It didn't matter that we didn't have any money. There are sick people in this world who wouldn't believe that.

Still, I might not have taken them seriously except that there had been some other strange incidents. One night while Jeb was away, I heard a car pull up in front of our house just as I was falling asleep. It was a few minutes after midnight. I got up but didn't turn on the light. As I watched, a second car pulled up behind the first. Two men got out of each car and stood at the end of our walk, talking to each other. Then they got back into their cars and raced off down the street.

A few minutes later they came back, parked at the curb again, got out and talked, and drove off again. It was eerie.

Then they came back a third time. They got out, talked, and went back to their cars. This time the second car pulled away so fast that the car went out of control and hit a tree. The driver fell forward onto the wheel, blowing the horn for several seconds.

By then I knew that every one of my neighbors was up and at a window, but no one turned on a light. Finally the man at the wheel sat up, backed his car away from the tree, and sped away.

I called the police to report the incident, but I knew what to expect. I had called them before. As soon as I identified myself, I was told that it wouldn't do any good for them to come out and investigate. The men were gone. If I insisted, they would come, but it would only mean more publicity and they knew I didn't want that.

"Don't you even want to see where the car hit the tree?" I said.

They didn't.

So when Jeb's lawyers told us there was always the possibility of a kidnaping, we believed them.

In April, just before Jeb went to the prosecutors, my father had three heart attacks. All his life he had been a robust, healthy man, but I know he was worried about us. He wasn't expected to live, yet he did. I don't know how I could have taken it if he hadn't.

Then, in May, just before Jeb was to testify before the Senate Committee, his mother died. We weren't ready for it. Jeb's mother was a vivacious, healthy woman who apparently was able to conceal her pain until the end. We had spoken to her on the phone only a few days before and she had sounded the same as ever—cheerful, encouraging, and well. When Jeb's brother Don called and told us she was "not feeling well," he knew what was wrong but didn't want to burden us with it. We had another call from Don a few days later. He said Jeb's mother was in the hospital, and he told Jeb he'd better come out to see her because "things didn't look good." We planned to leave on Monday. But the previous Saturday, at 3 o'clock in the morning, Don called and told Jeb his mother had died.

We made a quick trip to Santa Barbara for the funeral and then it was back to the Senate Committee. Jeb never had time to mourn. I could understand how he felt. Even though he knew cancer had killed his mother, he blamed himself—or the shame and anxiety he had caused her—for her death. It was irrational, but very human, and someday he would have to work that out in himself.

In many ways, it was difficult for us to have so much time before Jeb was sentenced. We just didn't know where we would be from one month to the next. People ask me how I managed to live each day with the prospect of prison and separation, but the truth is that I didn't face that prospect. I couldn't. I think Jeb was more realistic about it than I was. We talked about it, but only superficially. We never kept it from the children. But I could not accept the reality of it. In the back of my mind, there was always the hope that there would not be any prison sentence. Perhaps Jeb would be fined, I convinced myself. I wasn't concerned about being unable to pay a fine. We'd find a way. Somehow. And on and on I would go, allowing my thoughts to be led away from the one thing I could not face.

Still, I wouldn't have wanted any less time together. As it was, we were able to begin rebuilding our lives. Jeb was home with us much more than he had ever been, and it was a beautiful experience for all of us. We began to discover what was important in our lives.

I realized that even before the White House job there had been something wrong with the way we lived. Not that we were different from so many other families whose lifestyles were determined by careers. But that's just the point: the great foundation on which we tried to stand simply could not hold our weight.

It isn't right for a man—or a woman—to work during the hours that he ought to spend with his family. Long hours are not only destructive, but totally unnecessary. With a little planning, a little thought, a job can be done, and done well, within normal working hours. So many business trips accomplish nothing more than could be accomplished by telephone or letter.

Long working hours are fine, for a family who want to justify avoiding each other. But it seems to me that we are here on this earth to learn how to live together as human beings, and in our long working hours we create the kind of inanimate things—institutions and organizations—that stifle our humanity.

All along I had sensed this. Now I was sure of it. I know there are heavy demands on the time of many professional and business people, but unless they learn to control those demands, they and their families will be ruined by them. I could see it all around me—children alienated from their fathers, wives left to "bring up the kids" and resenting the responsibilities that had been dumped on them. I could identify with their loneliness. I knew why they were depressed, why they were drinking, why they were spending their time in idle gossip and bridge games. It saddened me to see some of them leave their already half-abandoned young children to get a job, but I could understand why they did it. They were trying to fill the emptiness that should have been filled by a spouse.

Our children needed their father as much as they needed me. And he needed them. They had always known how much they had loved each other, but now they were living each day around that love. There was time for them to talk—not in rushed sentences of the things that were practical and important at the moment, but in the slow, groping phrases that speak of our hopes and struggles and dreams. Nothing had to be marked "For Dad's Attention." Dad was there.

One of the good things about those fourteen months was a great big old Victorian house on several acres of land in Blue Ridge Summit, Pennsylvania. We needed to get away from Washington for a while, so we rented the house for a year. It was a good place for Jeb to work on his book, it was convenient for his business, and it had all the space we could possibly want. It was in a beautiful country setting, and the grounds were lovely. There was a funny old paddle tennis court in the back, which was great for paddle tennis and basketball games. With four active, healthy children, we needed it!

We did a lot of things together. We swam and sat in the sun and took long walks and played ball. At night, it was good to feel exhausted physically instead of emotionally, and in the morning, I relished waking up to the sound of birds instead of murmurs at the curb. Underneath the pressure and the anxiety of asking ourselves what was going to happen to us, something strong and warm was beginning to pull us together in a way we had never quite known. We were a family.

As I looked back over the past year, I was grateful that Jeb and I had not come to the point of divorce. How devastating it would have been for us and the children. And what good would it have accomplished? Jeb and I had chosen each other to share life together. There were certain things about each other that we had loved. Living together, we had found other things in each other that were not always lovable. That's the way life is. That's the way people are. The trouble is, when we go into marriage, we expect everything to be wedding-cake perfect, always beautiful. Most of us aren't prepared to love the whole person, faults and all. Jeb and I had been able to overlook our faults during most of the years we had been married. But during that past year, fear and guilt had pushed the lovable part of ourselves into the background. Now we were beginning to find it again. It was good and strong and wonderful. That, rather than something big and impersonal outside us, was what we would try to build our lives on.

Jeb's work with the prosecutors was done, at least for a while. He would be needed again before the trial, but we didn't know when that would be. He wanted to be able to plan his future, and so, in January, he asked that he be sentenced. The date was finally set for May 22 ,1974.

It was a hot day and we were back in Washington. Jeb's lawyers went with us to the courthouse. Our minister, Dr. Louis Evans, Jr., also went with us. The press were outside the courthouse, waiting for us. Cameras weren't allowed inside. We made our way through them, flashbulbs going off all around us, and Jeb promised them a statement when he came out.

People tell me I looked composed. I was in a daze. Madly, I allowed the possibility that there might not be a prison sentence to career around my mind.

As Jeb and his lawyers stood to receive the sentence, I held onto Louie Evans's hand so hard that my fingernails dug into him. I remember thinking how I must be hurting him, but there was nothing I could do to loosen my grip. He didn't wince. He just let me hold onto him.

I heard the words—ten months to four years in prison—and I was afraid I would either faint or become hysterical. I did neither. In fact I felt strangely calm, almost numb. It was some form of shock. Someone took my arm and guided me toward Jeb. The same thing had happened to him. He looked the way he always did, except for his eyes. We heard reporters rushing out of the courtroom. We heard familiar voices and when we turned toward the spectators' seats, we saw the faces of neighbors and friends who had come to be with us. We hadn't expected that. Later, much later, when we could begin to feel again, we would be grateful for their love. But we saw them through a cloud of disbelief. It was a stiff sentence.

There was a bit of sick humor, too. As Jeb and I started for the door on the side of the courtroom nearest us, a policeman stopped us and said, "No, not this door. He doesn't have to go to jail yet." On the other side of that door was the D.C. lockup.

Louie went to get the car and meet us out front. There was still the press to go through, and they were waiting for us on the other side of the big glass doors in front of the building. We opened the doors and were enveloped by microphones, cameras, and an impassable crush of bodies. As Jeb made his statement, a man squeezed through the crowd until he reached my side. "Here," he said in a hoarse whisper, pushing something at me, "here's my card. Call me. I must get your story." I tried to pull away from him, but there was no room. I shook my head angrily. Someone jostled his arm and the card fell to the ground.

The car was at the curb and Jeb's lawyers helped us into it. I don't know who drove us home. Everything was drowned out by the awful scream inside me that no one else could hear.

"Oh, God! Dear God! Help us!"

5

SOMEONE HAD HEARD. During those months I had often cried out to God, sometimes pleading like a hurt child, sometimes hysterically, choking on my tears. I don't know what I expected. A clap of thunder? Some kind of visible message etched in lightning? A miraculous erasure of everything that had gone wrong?

Perhaps. Nothing like that happened.

But someone heard. And someone knew—long before we did—that there would be an ordeal. Even before we had to face it, he began to prepare us for it. He didn't use thunder or lightning or a reshuffling of events. He used people—and love.

As soon as Jeb finished testifying before the Senate Committee, we began receiving letters from hundreds of people all over the country. They were so different from the articles and editorials in newspapers and magazines which denounced Jeb as some kind of a monster. These letters were kind, encouraging, helpful. They expressed appreciation for Jeb's courage in testifying, forgiveness for the wrong he had done and the hope that we would be able to build a good new life for ourselves. Suddenly we couldn't wait to get the mail each day! Page by page, the letters were lifting us up out of the gutter. Many were from Christians who wrote that they were praying for us. Some sent us Bibles.

One of the letters came from Colleen Townsend Evans, whose husband, Louie Evans, Jr., had been called to serve as Senior Pastor at National Presbyterian Church in Washington. The Evanses had just arrived from La Jolla, California, in the spring of 1973, and were moving into their new home on one of the days Jeb was testifying. Colleen wanted to follow the hearings and turned on the television set while the moving men were still bringing in their furniture—and she saw Jeb. When he finished his testimony Colleen dug through their unpacked cartons to find some stationery and sent us a letter we will always cherish. She also thought we might feel like talking to someone—they would be there if we needed them. We noticed from their return address that they lived only a few blocks away.

One summer evening while the children and I were in Blue Ridge Summit and Jeb was home alone, he drove over to the Evanses to thank them for their kindness. That was the beginning of a wonderful friendship and an education in the meaning of Christian living.

Jeb told me about Louie and Colleen Evans, and when we went back to Washington, we attended a service at National Presbyterian Church. It was a beautiful experience for us. We were just two people who walked into a house filled with God's love. No one stared. No one nudged. No one whispered behind a discreet hand. We were welcomed. We were warmed. We had found a church home.

Jeb and I had always gone to church. Even before we were married—when I was a student at the University of California at Berkeley and Jeb had his first real job in San Francisco—we used to go out on Saturday night and then meet each other Sunday morning for church. Wherever we lived, we always had a home church—until we came to Washington. In the four years we had lived there, we had drifted from church to church, never feeling as if we really belonged to any of them. We kept up our attendance because it seemed like the "right" thing to do, and we wanted our children to have a Christian education.

Until recently everything about our lives had been "right." To some people we were like a storybook couple—the handsome man and the pretty lady who got married and lived happily ever after—and I think we believed that about ourselves. Even our children were "right." When they were babies they were never too fat or too thin. They were beautiful and healthy and full of humor.

Everything we did turned out well. Jeb always had an exciting job. We had a lovely home and we made friends easily. Bad things just didn't happen to us. With all the traveling we did, there never was an accident, hardly even a close call. We seldom were sick. People used to tell us we brightened their day.

Naturally we loved God. He was the one who gave us all those good things. And we loved his world—the sun on the beaches, the cool shade of the trees, the mountains rising up into a sky that seemed to be blue just for us. Loving God was like loving ourselves. When we worshiped him, we were rejoicing in the sense of power he seemed to share with us. We were members of the same club.

We knew very little about Jesus Christ. We spoke his name and acknowledged that he was the Son of God. But we didn't *know* him. Savior was a word in a hymnbook, quaint and charming, but not something we use today. Who needed to be saved? From what? Nonsense! We were on top of the world.

Suddenly we hit bottom—over and over and over again. The power was gone and we were completely helpless. We didn't even know how to reach out for God because we never expected to be in such circumstances. Would he be there? Or would he be off somewhere, smiling and letting the sun shine on some other storybook couple? Would he even want anything to do with people like us? Over those months, as time and time again I cried out to him, I was slowly learning about my personal need for a real—and two-way—relationship with God.

But then there were the letters. And the warmth of our reception at church. Ever so slowly the veil was being lifted from my eyes. God didn't only love us when everything we did turned out well. *He loved us!*

In the fall of that year, Colleen Evans brought together the first covenant group in our church and invited me to join her and several other women in a special form of ministry. I said yes immediately, without really knowing why or what I was joining. But something told me this was what I needed. We met once each week, sometimes to study the Bible and sometimes just to talk. Gradually we opened our lives to each other. We shared each other's pain and joy. We prayed for each other and helped each other in our times of need.

Whatever we said in our group was confidential, but even though we knew we could trust each other it was a long time before some of us could speak freely. I was one of the slow ones. I wasn't accustomed to being in need. I also found it difficult to verbalize my feelings, partly because they were so confused and partly because I had never done it before.

It helped to hear women who were mature Christians praising the Lord right in the middle of a crisis. At first, I didn't understand how they could do it. Was it hypocritical? Then the veil was lifted a little more. I saw that they were praising God for his nearness, for the help they knew they could count on him to give. They were praising him for the crisis itself because it gave them the opportunity to experience his healing powers. They knew God! Truly knew him—because they knew his son. And so they could sincerely say, "Praise the Lord!" in the midst of trouble.

If I had never been in that covenant group, I might have believed I was the only person in the world who was suffering as I did. But through these wonderful women, I learned that others were suffering too, some even more than I. For some reason our group was beset by crisis after crisis—the death of a brother, the near death of a child, a radical mastectomy, the pain of a broken relationship. I watched these women reach out to a God I realized I had never known—and I saw them healed. They weren't perfect creatures. They were human beings, just like me. Their God was equal to any circumstance, any pain. Surely he would help me.

Then I *really* began to understand. Left to our own resources, we all make a mess of our lives. It wasn't power that Jeb and I had had before. It was delusion. We had always been helpless when it came to doing something right with our lives. And now we couldn't possibly straighten ourselves out. That's what Jesus Christ was all about.

He wasn't just a name to me anymore. Christmas wasn't just a birthday party, nor was Easter a solemn occasion marking a death. It all began to fit together. Jesus was a person, the most real person I would ever know. He was born to do the straightening out we couldn't do for ourselves. A letter or a message wouldn't have served the purpose. He had to come in person. He had to be here, where we are, so that he could stand in our shoes, take our sins upon himself, and then take our place upon the cross. Only he was big enough to do that. Only he could do battle with the evil in us. And only he could overcome it. God loved us that much!

Saved—now it was more than a buzzword to me. Yes, I had sinned—and I would sin again. So would Jeb, and so would we all, to a greater or lesser degree. But that wasn't the end of our story. We didn't have to be the prisoners of our sins. We didn't have to wear them, like chains around our legs, for the rest of our lives. The penalty had already been paid—for all time—by the man on the cross. If we could accept who he was and accept what he had done, we were free. We could turn in our sins—to him!

Jeb also had joined a covenant group, and together we

began to read our Bible—seriously, for the first time. It was difficult, and we read slowly. We were hungry for meaning.

One day in the spring of 1974, I ran into Joanne Kemp, the wife of Congressman Jack Kemp of New York, whom I hadn't seen for a long time. I met her in the supermarket where I always did my shopping, but I had never seen her there before. She didn't live in the neighborhood, and, at that time, neither one of us knew why she was there at that particular hour. (I understand who sent her now.) I didn't notice her because I was preoccupied and troubled, but she called my name and we stopped to talk. She asked me how things were going, and I told her they weren't going well at all.

The following week, I met Joanne again in the same store. She told me she was taking a course called Bible Study Fellowship and asked me if I would like to come with her to one of the meetings. Again, something told me that was what I needed, and I said yes. I didn't know it then, but that was another way God was preparing me for what lay ahead.

The course on the Gospel of John lasted for six weeks, but I was able to attend only three of the meetings. They were wonderful. Our teacher, Lee Campbell, held 350 women spellbound with her insight and her teaching. At her suggestion, we supplemented the King James Version with one of the modern translations, and I found *The Living Bible* very helpful. Suddenly the Bible was no longer a blur. Not only was it clear, but relevant. God was saying something to me—and to every other person in that room.

That fall, the first full nine-month session of Bible Study Fellowship was conducted in the Washington area, and because our group was new, we were assigned to study the Letters of Paul. Students in other parts of the country were reading the Minor Prophets. I couldn't help feeling that this was another expression of God's mercy. Someday I would be ready for the Minor Prophets, but, at that moment, I needed to know more about Jesus Christ. And who could tell me better than Paul writing from a prison cell?

I can't say that there was any one moment when Christ came into my life because he came to me in so many different ways. First I felt the warmth of his love. Symbols of it were all around me. I knew that he gave me his love without any strings attached, and, while I understood that intellectually, it took me a long time to feel it deep inside myself. He didn't ask me to be different, yet somehow I *wanted* to be. That's when I realized Jesus was more than a presence. He was a guide.

I wasn't trying to be a good girl and get straight A's as a Christian. I just looked at my life through different eyes. Slowly, in many ways, I began to change. It wasn't anything people could see on the outside. But inside I felt something new beginning to grow in me.

So many of our expectations had been shattered. The rules that once guided our lives and our behavior had turned out to be only flimsy fences that gave way when we leaned against them. It had been a long fall to the bottom and for months we lay there, stunned. Now it was time to move on, but certainly not in the same direction.

We felt that we could no longer accept anyone—even each other—as a stereotype. We had to deal with people as they really were. That made a tremendous difference in our relationship with each other and with our children.

How could I ask my children to live up to some preconceived image of what a good child should be? Who gave me that image in the first place? And did that person even know my child? Did I? Was I, as a mother, and was Jeb, as a father, helping each of our children to be himself or herself? Or were we trying to turn out superior Barbie dolls?

For instance, our son Justin is an intelligent, inventive child who can create wonderful things. He has been doing that since he was very young. I remember when we got a color TV set, he couldn't wait for us to unpack it—not because he wanted to watch TV, but because he wanted the huge cardboard box the set came in. He took it down to our basement and turned it into a "computerized" answer box by cutting slots in it and wiring it with Christmas tree lights. Inside he put a tiny chair, the full set of the *World Book Encyclopedia*, and a pad and pencil. When the lights were on, that meant the computer was working and anyone in the neighborhood could write a question on a piece of paper, put it in a slot, and, within a few minutes, the answer would come out on a piece of paper pushed through another slot. Justin was only ten years old when he did that.

But Justin's room was always a shambles, and if I asked him to go upstairs and put away some of the things that lay on the floor, chances were he never got there. Later I would find him sitting on the stairs, busily drawing something on a piece of paper. He had completely forgotten what I asked him to do. That used to drive me up the wall. But now I saw my child in a totally different way. He didn't have to fit into a mold. He didn't have to be what I wanted him to be. He was himself, and I was beginning to accept him that way—just as God accepted me. I saw a charming, inventive child with a marvelous ability to create something beautiful out of nothing—and a lovably irritating way of forgetting some things that may not have been as important as I once thought they were. To me that was an amazing discovery.

Both Stuart and Tracy, our youngest children, were dyslexic, which meant they had slight reading problems. That was something Jeb and I used to find hard to accept. We wanted our children to be outstanding in *every* way, just as we had tried to be. We wanted the flaws and the problems not to be there, so we tried to minimize them. Now we knew better. To be human is to be flawed. Once we could accept imperfection in ourselves, we could accept it in our children. And we loved them even more.

Perhaps there would be a new life for us. We couldn't be sure. So much of the future was uncertain and we still lived each day with so many values from the past. In the old Victorian house in Pennsylvania, we felt close and strengthened by a deeper love than we had ever felt. We were nourished in our new church. Our mailbox had become a messenger of good will. But what would happen if Jeb went to prison?

On the way home after he was sentenced, I was my old self again—frightened, pleading for help, and not sure I was going to get it. All the warmth and love and understanding seemed to have gone out of my life, and I felt terribly alone.

6

THERE WERE TWELVE DAYS left before Jeb had to go to prison. We had hoped to have the time to ourselves, but so many things began to happen at once.

Jeb's book was scheduled to come out any day and already it was in some of the bookstores. We would need the money to support us while Jeb was in prison, so it was important to us to sell as many copies as we could. His publisher was eager to promote it and wanted to use Jeb as much as he could. Would we do *The Dick Cavett Show?* May 31, the Friday before Jeb was to leave for Allenwood Prison Camp, was Prize Day at Whitney's school. It was one of the most important events of the year and we didn't want to miss it. Friends and neighbors wanted to say good-bye.

I didn't want to do the Cavett show at all. I had never watched it, so I had nothing against it as a program. I just didn't want any more exposure, especially at such a sensitive time. Jeb disagreed. He felt, as he always did, that people in the news and public relations media had a job to do. He also reminded me that we would have to deal with them anyway, and he thought it was better to cooperate. Somewhere in my mind, I knew he was right about the fact that we had to deal with them, but I resented his willingness to allow us to be used on their behalf. I still do. Perhaps I was irrational, but rationality was not the name of the game anyone was playing then.

I hurt too much to worry about how someone did his job. I was too concerned about what prison would do to my husband and what his absence would mean to our children.

When Jeb's publishers assured us that Dick Cavett was "the gentleman of TV," I gave in, although I was going against my better judgment. Then we learned that the Cavett people wanted to tape the interview in our home. I was appalled at the idea. Barbara Walters had interviewed me in my kitchen a few months earlier, but that was different. My husband wasn't going into prison in a few days then.

"But you'll be so much more comfortable in your own home," everyone kept saying. I had too many other things on my mind and finally I said yes. In the state I was in, I might have agreed to anything.

Near the end of Jeb's last week at home, he and I managed to get away together. We hadn't been able to keep Alicia on a fulltime basis, but now and then, when we needed her, she was able to take care of the children. We spent a few wonderful days at a friend's apartment in Rehoboth Beach, Delaware—not far from home, but a world apart in environment. It was quiet. There were only the two of us. We lay on the beach in the sun and played tennis. In the evening, we kept our door open to the cool breezes. We could hear the waves breaking regularly, and something about that rhythm soothed us. We needed to be reminded that the world was not going to end.

And in still another way God prepared us for what was coming. We turned on the *Today Show* one morning, something we seldom did other weekdays. But this time we didn't have the distractions of Jeb going off to work and the children going to school. We had the time to watch and listen. One of the guests was Lynn Caine, author of the book *Widow*, and as she began to speak, I called Jeb, who was in the bathroom, shaving, and asked him to listen.

Jeb was so much more realistic than I was! Immediately

he realized that I was going to feel like a widow when he left for prison and he wanted me to be ready for the shock. At first I shrank back from the idea. I didn't want to be ready—not yet. But I listened, and as I did tears came to my eyes. I was touched by my husband's compassion. How helpless he must be feeling. He had always made the decisions in our family. He was the one who took care of us all. How was he going to feel being cut off from us, knowing that if the roof fell in he wouldn't be there to hold it up somehow. To a man like Jeb, that was a special agony.

Mrs. Caine had been through it all, and as I watched I felt as if she were speaking directly to me, telling me about the different emotional stages I was about to go through. In a sense, Jeb and I had experienced a death, a shattering of everything we had believed in. Our trust in our system of government and in justice itself had been destroyed. It *was* better to know, ahead of time, that I would be numb at first, that I would go through everything with apparent ease. I was beginning to do that already. And then there would be the gradual—or even sudden—awareness of pain. There would be loneliness to such a degree that I would want to curl up and die. There would also be—if I tried hard enough—a deliberate involvement in new interests and new friends.

"Thank you, Lord, for Lynn Caine," I prayed silently. Then I realized that her husband would not be coming back —ever. "And bless her, Lord!" I prayed again. As soon as I had the chance I bought her book. Reading it was like being with a friend who really understood.

We returned home on Thursday, May 30. When we drove up to our house, I couldn't believe what I saw. There at the curb was a huge forty-foot moving van disconnected from its cab and set up on mounts. Long black cables about an inch in diameter ran from the van up the lawn and into the front door, which was ajar. Several men went in and out of the house while we watched. *The Dick Cavett Show* had arrived.

Inside it was worse. The thick black cables ran through our first-floor rooms like serpents. They were on the floor and taped to the walls. Equipment of all kinds was strewn throughout the living room, dining room, and kitchen. The den was filled with supplies. I wondered if they had spared our bedroom, which was also on the first floor. Fortunately they had.

I hadn't expected anything like this. When Barbara Walters came, she brought a cameraman, a technician, and her secretary, that was all. She walked in, looked through some of our rooms, and decided to interview me in the kitchen. It took about an hour to set up, an hour to interview, and another hour to put my house back in order.

Our walls were newly painted, and I winced at the sight of the heavy black tape holding up those cables. What would happen when the tape was pulled away? The Dick Cavett interview was scheduled for 4 o'clock the next afternoon. How were we going to live in our house until then?

Betty Ann Besch, the producer of the show, was there. We had met her when she came to our house a few days before we went to Rehoboth Beach. She had spent several hours talking to us, getting "background" for the interview.

For the next day the house was a mob scene. Technicians came and went. Neighborhood children, fascinated by the unusual activity, peered in our first-floor windows and followed the technicians around, asking questions about the equipment. Every dog in the neighborhood visited us because the front door could not be closed. It was awfully hot, but it made no sense to turn on the air conditioner as long as the door was open.

In the midst of it all, a Montgomery County policeman came to our door asking for Jeb. Jeb was out, so he walked through the rooms until he found me in the kitchen. Lifting his voice above the noise he told me he had a warrant for Jeb's arrest. I stared at him. Had the whole world gone insane?

He repeated what he had said. Then he explained that

our car had been issued a parking ticket months ago and no fine had been paid. He had come to collect the twelve dollars or arrest the owner of the car.

Suddenly I remembered. I was the one who got the ticket. I was parked in downtown Bethesda and when I came back to the car the meter had run out and there was a ticket on my windshield. It had happened before. Usually I paid the fine immediately and that was the end of it. This time I had forgotten. It was in the midst of the Senate Committee hearings and the last thing on my mind was a parking ticket. I don't even know what happened to the ticket. I guess I lost it.

Didn't his man *know?* He was too late. My husband was already going to prison! Or did the police want to be sure they collected the fine before Jeb slipped through their fingers?

I became hysterical. I stood there screaming at him, asking him why the police hadn't come when reporters banged on our door late at night. Why hadn't they come when strange cars pulled up in front of our house at midnight?

Finally he seemed to understand. This was not the time to track down a missing parking ticket. Embarrassed and, I think, a little frightened by my hysteria, he left quickly after I wrote him a check for twelve dollars.

Jeb's lawyers had arranged for him to enter prison after Prize Day at St. Albans. Whit had made the honor roll and Jeb wanted to be there when his name was read. The ceremonies took place on Friday at 11 o'clock in the morning.

Early that afternoon, one of Whitney's friends called and invited him to come to a party at his house. Ordinarily Whit would have gone. School was over and there was a holiday feeling in the air. But I heard him say, "No—my father is going to prison Tuesday, so I want to be with him the next few days." I loved him so. What courage it took for a thirteen-year-old-boy to say that!

Dick Cavett arrived at 3:30, a half hour before the taping was to begin. The house was too hot for him so he stayed in his air-conditioned limousine until five minutes before the taping. We all exchanged a few meaningless remarks and went out to our backyard to begin. Within a few minutes, we were back inside. There was too much humidity and too much noise from the planes overhead. By this time both Jeb and Dick Cavett had their jackets off.

The interview was a horrible experience. I couldn't believe that this was "the gentleman of TV." It didn't seem to me that he used any of Betty Ann's "background" material. He spent most of the time insisting that he never would have done the kind of things Jeb had done. He knew, he said, he could never sink that low. He seemed to have no awareness that he was in our home—and that Jeb's children were present.

Later we received a lot of mail from viewers who saw that show. Most of them felt that Dick Cavett had made a fool of himself by setting himself up as a god.

The paint did come off the wall when they pulled off the tape holding up the cables, but our painter was able to patch it up. In putting things back, someone broke a decoupage lamp I had made for Jeb one Christmas. That was irreplaceable.

The last Sunday we spent together in our home was a strange mixture of joy and sadness. Our friends and neighbors, the Gillespies, made it a joy. The sadness came from the fact that we could not be sure when we all would be together again. Perhaps in ten months, when Jeb had served the minimum part of his sentence—but that was only a "perhaps." None of us really knew.

We had a lovely dinner at the Gillespies' house that Sunday. The Gillespies have five children and they, along with our own, kept us from somber thoughts. Then, when it was time for us to go home, the children threw their arms around Jeb and hugged him as hard as they could. "Good-bye, Uncle Jeb," they kept saying, almost pulling him down with their affection. Joan and Gilly Gillespie held us tightly and we could see that they were trying just as hard as we were not to cry.

A few minutes after we got home, the Gillespie children came over to give Jeb another hug. And then they came back again, this time with little notes they had written for him.

Jeb was assigned to Allenwood Prison in Pennsylvania. It was supposed to be the "best prison around." Our lawyers told us it was labeled "a country club prison" because the inmates slept in dormitories instead of cells and the guards didn't carry guns. It was about four hours away by car in the rolling hills of Pennsylvania.

Originally Jeb was supposed to be escorted to prison—in handcuffs and leg irons, with a chain around his waist—by federal marshals. His lawyers, however, were able to convince the judge that the customary precautions would not be necessary. Jeb had turned himself in when he went to the prosecutors. He had been around for fourteen months, so obviously he wasn't going to run away now. He would turn himself in at prison, too. I thanked God for this new mercy. I don't know what I would have done if I—or, worse than that, our children —had seen Jeb in irons. In my protected life I had never learned about such things, and I shudder for all the men and women who have to endure that humiliation.

We decided to take our time getting to Allenwood. We left Monday morning and stayed overnight at the Hershey Hotel, a lovely old inn with magnificent gardens. The weather was beautiful, warm enough for Jeb to have a swim in the hotel pool that afternoon. Some of the guests recognized us and stopped to say hello. One kind woman impulsively gave Jeb a souvenir mug she had just received at a convention banquet.

It was a strange time for us. Part of us was enjoying the scenery and quiet relaxation of the hotel, and part of us had stopped feeling anything. I remember listening intently at dinner as Jeb went over our finances with me, explaining his schedule for paying bills, but I didn't really comprehend any of it. Not that it was beyond my understanding. I just didn't want to think about being without him. He told me when I should take the car in for a tune-up, where I should take it, and how much it was likely to cost. Soon it would be time for the children to go to camp, and it would be up to me to decide whether we could afford it. Later, his instructions would come back to me, but, at that moment, I did not know how I was going to let him go. Was I really going to drive my husband to prison and go home alone?

We had been told what to expect from prison, but most of the information was wrong. We thought that a "country club prison" meant Jeb could wear his own clothes if he wanted to, that he could come home on weekend "furloughs," and sometimes I would be allowed to take him out to a restaurant on visiting day. Jeb's lawyers—and many other lawyers—actually believed that. They have never been to prison, so how would they know the truth? They were like most of the public—Jeb and me included—who simply did not want to look into that dark part of our civilization.

Fortunately we learned a few hard facts before Jeb had to leave. Through his lawyers, he was put in touch with a former inmate of Allenwood. One day, we met him for lunch and he had the courage to be brutally honest.

"Don't bring anything with you," he said, "because they won't let you take it in with you. Don't wear a watch—except maybe a cheap Timex. Man, you walk in naked—empty!"

Not even some books? we asked. Couldn't Jeb bring a Bible and a few other books?

"Well, maybe," he said. "Take a few books along with you, and if the guard is in a good mood that day, he might let you bring them in."

But there would be no furloughs, no dinners outside the

prison grounds. And Jeb would wear army surplus clothing. "Don't bring any underwear. Not even your toothbrush!"

We believed him. On Tuesday morning when we left the hotel, Jeb had only the clothes on his back and a small cardboard box containing a Bible and a few books.

We stopped for lunch in Lewisburg. There wasn't much time left. Allenwood was only a few miles away.

We arrived during visiting hours, a little before 3 in the afternoon. The reporters were there at the gate. More flashbulbs and another interview. Then we were inside.

The prison is in the middle of nowhere, which is true of most prisons. But this one was surrounded by some of the loveliest scenery in the East. During June in Pennsylvania, everything is green and leafy. The prison buildings were one story high, made of brick—everything very neat, but sterile. There was no landscaping, only dirt, in the area to which the prisoners were confined.

We parked in front of the Administration Building. Outside on a patio there were a lot of prisoners and their visitors. They knew who we were and they stared. We walked past them into the building. We were in a large, noisy, hot reception room where there were more prisoners and visitors. There were vending machines for ice cream, coffee, soda, candy, and pizza. The air was heavy with the odors of cigarette smoke, spilled vending machine food, and dirty restrooms. A few babies were crying, and some of the children were cajoling coins for the machines. People watched and did not speak.

Jeb checked in with the guard at the desk. He said he would be back in a few minutes and then left with another guard.

I did not see anyone, although several people—inmates and visitors—approached me quietly, trying to comfort me. I heard sounds and I smelled the incredible odors of that room, but they did not register except in some far corner of my mind. Later—days and weeks later—they would come back to me so that over and over I would find myself walking into that room for the first time, no matter where I was.

I don't know how long Jeb was gone. Three-fifteen came and the visitors left, but the guard at the desk said I could stay a little longer.

There he was. I saw Jeb coming from a room somewhere in the back of the building. Yes, it was Jeb—but no, it wasn't. Then I saw it was his clothes that made him look so strange. Everything was khaki-colored, just like the other prisoners we had seen. But nothing fit. The shirt was wrinkled and torn. The pants came to several inches above his ankles. The shoes were black and looked as if they were made of cardboard. They were stiff and much too big and I could see Jeb's foot coming through one of the sides. He looked as if someone had dressed him up to play a clown in some sort of devilish comedy. It wasn't funny, it was cruel.

He was ashamed. I saw the pain in his eyes and knew he was wishing I weren't there.

There were no last tender moments. There were only muttered sentences that said nothing of what we were feeling. We hugged each other and kissed each other quickly with the guard looking on impassively. Then I left.

I didn't cry. I went out to the car, started it and drove away. I seemed to do everything mechanically, with great ease.

I drove for four hours until I reached home. I had been worried about the trip back, wondering whether I would lose my way. I didn't. It was a truck route, and ordinarily that would have bothered me. The road was narrow—alternating between two and three lanes most of the way. But then, I wasn't the one who was doing the driving that day. God did it for me.

There was a PTA meeting that night and I had planned to attend it. As soon as I reached home the phone rang. It was Joan Gillespie.

"Come on over," she said.

"No, I can't," I said. "I have to go to a PTA meeeting."

"Well, come over and then go to the meeting," she said.

How strange, I thought as I walked across the street, *I'm not coming apart.* I didn't feel anything. I spent a half hour with Joan and then she decided to come along with me to the meeting, which by then had become a mountain I was determined to scale. Somehow, if I could get through that meeting and prove to myself that everything was perfectly normal, I would be all right. I would be able to take care of my children.

Many times I have looked back to that night, wondering what people thought when they saw me walk into a PTA meeting. It really wouldn't have mattered if I had known. I was completely surrounded—insulated—by Joan, her children, and my four children. I don't remember a thing about the meeting itself. That wasn't important. What mattered was the fact that I was able to go through the motions.

Lynn Caine was right. The first thing you feel when you lose your husband—is that *you don't feel.*

7

I TOOK OUR CHILDREN with me when I visited Jeb at Allenwood each weekend. I saw no reason why I shouldn't. We had been honest with them about the reason their father had to go to prison, and we felt it was better for them to see him there, as it really was, than to imagine what it was like. Besides, we needed every opportunity to be together as a family.

Visiting hours were from 8:30 to 3:15 every day. If we had gone during the week, we could have visited Jeb two days in a row, but on weekends, inmates could have visitors either Saturday or Sunday, not both. There was no reason for the rule. Like so many other things about prison life, it simply existed.

I wanted the children to be able to see their friends as much as possible during the week, so we usually left for Allenwood on Friday morning, and came back Saturday night.

The first time we went was the Friday after Jeb entered prison. We were very nervous. I had been told—or perhaps I had read it somewhere—that our first visit would be the crucial one, because a man who goes to prison is afraid his wife and children will reject him. Our behavior would be very important.

"Daddy's going to need a lot of loving," I told the children as I drove. "So don't hold back. Give him plenty of

c

hugs." I really didn't have to prompt them. They loved their father and they missed him terribly already.

They were good kids. It was hot in the car and four hours is a long time for children to sit still. We played alphabet games with the letters on passing license plates and we made up quizzes. When we got to Harrisburg, we stopped at a Howard Johnson's for a milkshake and before we got back in the car I told the children to run around the building several times. The exercise helped relax the tension that was building up in them.

I had no way of knowing how our children would react to seeing Jeb as I last saw him. Each one was so different. Whitney was thirteen and very responsible. I knew he wouldn't want to cry. Justin at eleven was realizing that he wasn't a child anymore. Deep feelings would be hard for him to handle. Tracy, at ten, was beginning to take after me. She kept her feelings to herself, but I knew they were there. And little Stuart was seven. He had a special need for Jeb because he was too young to understand why his father didn't come home anymore.

I felt so empty-handed. Visitors weren't allowed to bring anything to eat or drink, so all I could bring was a lot of coins for the vending machines. I wasn't happy about the kind of food the children would have to eat, but it was better than nothing, and they were sure to get hungry while we were there.

We arrived a few minutes after one o'clock. The guard at the reception desk asked to see my driver's license. Then he asked for the make of my car and the license number. I had never memorized the number, so Whit ran out and got it. The guard looked through my shopping bag and saw that it contained only some mail and a few games and books for the children. He told us to sit down and wait while he called the dormitory and told Jeb he had visitors.

We were hot and felt dirty from the ride, so while we waited, we went into the restrooms and cleaned ourselves up as well as we could. We couldn't get out of them fast enough. Then we sat and waited.

The first thing I noticed about Jeb when I saw him was that he was perspiring heavily, which was unusual for him. His face was wet. He was pale and his eyes were glazed. He came toward us slowly, stiffly, as if he were made of wood. Fortunately the children didn't wait. As soon as he was past the guard, they threw themselves at him, hugging and kissing him and talking all at once. I felt their need for him and I smiled, seeing them together. But Jeb didn't respond. He couldn't even lift his arms away from his sides. He couldn't smile or laugh or say a word. He just stood there, letting the children cling to him. His feelings were so strong that I think he was afraid of breaking down in front of us.

I put my arms around him and kissed him. His body was cold. If the children noticed how dazed he was, it didn't seem to matter. They took his hands and led him outside where the air was cooler and smelled fresher, talking constantly and happily. When Jeb sat down, Stuart climbed on his lap and there he stayed with his arms around Jeb's neck for most of the rest of the day. He had a special need to touch his father.

It took Jeb about forty-five minutes to relax and begin to talk. If we had been concerned about this visit, how must he have felt? I took his hand and it was warm. His face was dry.

The khakis Jeb wore that day fit him better and they weren't full of holes. The shoes weren't open at the sides, but, still, they were strange-looking.

I opened my shopping bag and gave Jeb the mail to read. I let the children dig in the bag to find whatever interested them, and I gave Jeb the handful of change I had collected and he put it in his pocket. That way, when the children wanted something from the vending machine they could get the money from their father just as they usually did.

The patio and the reception room were crowded with

people, the visitors mirroring the prison population in general. About 50 percent of the inmates came from the city ghettos. They were poor Puerto Ricans and blacks, and most of them were in on drug-use or minor fraud charges. Their wives looked tired and depressed. They did the best they could to control their children, and all of the children were surprisingly good. It was particularly hard for these women to get to Allenwood. Most of them didn't have their own cars and there was no public transportation available close to the prison, which meant that they had to wait until someone with a car could bring them. Obviously they couldn't visit every week; in fact, they couldn't even be certain when they could go at all. I knew, from Jeb, that many of these families were in serious financial trouble. In most cases, the husband had been the only source of income, and now that he was in prison, the only alternative was welfare. A job for these women was out of the question because their children were too young to be left alone, and the women were not trained to do anything that would pay them enough to cover the cost of a babysitter.

Inmates convicted of drug dealing made up about 40 percent of the Allenwood population. Others were members of organized crime—or "OC," as they referred to it—and admittedly Mafia-related. Their wives and children used to arrive in shiny new cars. The women were flamboyant but motherly, and more cheerful than the women from the ghettos. Most of them were heavy and suffered from the summer heat, so they wore as few clothes as possible and fanned themselves with magazines or their open hands as they sat with their men.

The rest of the inmates fell into the category marked "miscellaneous." Some were young draft resisters whose wives and girlfriends wore jeans or long cotton skirts and loose gauzy blouses. These women had a very casual attitude toward their children, and some nursed their babies without embarrassment in the reception room. Many of the "miscellaneous" prisoners were in on Medicare fraud or income-tax evasion. Some were doctors or businessmen; their wives drove station wagons and their children were in their teens. The women were quiet and troubled-looking; they were concerned about their children, some of whom were rebelling self-destructively in their reaction to their father's absence. I could identify with them in their anxiety because neither Jeb nor I could be sure how our own children would react.

Crowded as the visiting areas were, only a small percentage of the 430 prisoners at Allenwood had visitors. There were a number of reasons for this. Prisons aren't the kind of institutions "nice" people want in their neighborhood, so most of them are located in remote, inaccessible areas. Families often find it impossible to get to them at all; the trip is too long and too expensive. Many of those who make it can't keep doing it because the experience is too exhausting and depressing on top of the problems of caring for a family without the help of a husband or father. Divorce and desertion are common. And a lot of the men in prison just never had any family at all.

Prisoners who didn't have visitors were not allowed into the reception room or outside on the patio. They weren't allowed to use the vending machines. But they could pretend that they had to go to the mailroom, which was right next to the reception room and opened into it. A cluster of men stood there watching us. They looked lonely, and their presence was a constant reminder that there were things about prison far worse than I was experiencing.

I was beginning to feel the deep depression that marked the faces of everyone around us. Part of that first day, Jeb and I sat holding hands, wordlessly crying over the nightmare that had become our reality.

It was 3:15 and time to go. I gathered up our books and games and put them in the shopping bag. The children held onto Jeb for a moment, but they didn't protest. It was one of the many ways I was to learn about the wisdom of children.

"Good-bye, honey," I said, and kissed Jeb. We left him

in the reception room and walked out to the patio and down the stairs to the car. We didn't say a word to each other.

As I backed the car out of our parking space, I looked into the rearview mirror and saw Jeb standing on the patio watching us. He was crying. I watched him growing smaller and smaller in the mirror as I drove away. I could hardly see the road through my tears. Tracy began to cry quietly, turning her head away. Stuart sobbed in anger—"I don't want to leave Daddy there! I don't want to leave Daddy there!" Justin and Whitney fought to control themselves, caught between the child and the man inside themselves.

I thought of the weeks stretching out ahead of us. *Ten months*—at least. I didn't even try to pretend I could get through them. I *knew* I couldn't, and I was not ashamed to let my children see my weakness.

"Dear Lord," I prayed aloud, "we aren't strong enough for this. Make us stronger, Lord. I don't care how—but make us stronger!"

I cried most of the way to the Sheraton Inn where we stayed for the night. We ate dinner only because we knew we should, but none of us enjoyed it. I think we all cried ourselves to sleep that night.

During the next week, I had to face another problem— money. The money Jeb had earned as a consultant during those fourteen months, plus what was left of the advance on his book, would have to take care of our basic needs for the coming year, provided I was careful how I spent it. I was cutting back in every way I could, but there were two expenditures I wanted to be able to make—tuition for the children's school and summer camp for Whitney and Justin. To others that may have seemed extravagant, but to me they were essential. We felt that the Maryland public schools were no better than they had been four years earlier when we had moved there. They couldn't provide our children with the education they needed for their future lives. Besides, they had made many friends at their private schools, and they needed the security of those friendships. For the same reason we wanted the two older boys to go to summer camp. I wanted them to be challenged and active physically, as well as to be surrounded by adult male counselors. Without camp, they would face a very lonely summer, and they were carrying enough of a burden without that.

So—I had to economize in other areas, which I didn't mind. After all, we weren't going hungry or doing without anything we really needed. Even financially, God had provided for us ahead of time. But we couldn't afford to stay at a motel every weekend when we visited Jeb.

I decided to try to make the trip in one day, which meant eight hours of driving. It was a foolish thing to do, but at the time it seemed to make sense. If I had to get stronger—well, this was one of the ways to do it.

The next Friday, we left very early in the morning and I drove hard at high speeds all the way. I thought I would have enough time to rest while we were visiting Jeb, but I had forgotten how exhausting that experience was. When we left, I cried all the way to the car. There was no way I could hold back my tears, nor did I want to. Little by little I was learning to be open about my feelings, and if that caused me some discomfort, that was the way it had to be.

It was about 3:15 when we started for home, and for a while I thought I was doing pretty well. I didn't realize that I was just plain psyched up.

There is one thirty-mile stretch of road I had already learned to dread. It had only one lane in each direction, so I had to pull out into the left lane in order to pass other cars. Usually I took my time and didn't try to pass anything until we reached a wider part of the road, but, on that day, I was in a hurry to get home. I looked ahead in the oncoming lane and saw a truck coming toward us quite far off in the distance. Yes, I could make it, I decided, and pulled out into the left lane. As soon as I got there I realized that I had misjudged. The truck was much closer than I had thought and was barreling down on us. My reaction time told me how tired I really was. I seemed to sit there at the wheel forever and then finally I pushed my foot down on the accelerator, jerked the car ahead and back into the right lane in front of the car I was passing—just in time! The truck whizzed past, its huge wheels blurred.

I was sick with fear. In my mind I could see Jeb being summoned to the Administration Building where he would be told that his family had been wiped out. I hadn't considered that before. I was only thinking about the expense of the trip. Now I knew I had a much more important responsibility. I had to keep our family safe.

I drove slowly until we came to the three-lane part of the road again and then I pulled off the road by an overpass. I told the children to get out of the car and stretch their legs while I took a rest. Underneath the overpass and out of sight of the road, I lay down on the concrete and let myself go limp. I stayed there until I knew I was in control of myself again.

So much for getting strong, I thought. I couldn't wait for God to strengthen me—I had to do it myself. But who said I was supposed to be the strong one, anyway? Not God. I had forgotten. There were no strings attached to his love for me. If I had my weaknesses, that was okay with him. He had enough strength for both of us.

I was still a little shy about asking Jesus for anything. I seemed to feel that I ought to save that for something critical. But who was I to decide what was a crisis and what was not? I had been trying to save a few dollars and I almost killed us all!

"All right, Jesus, I think I understand," I said. "I can't handle this situation. But *you* can—and we need your help. However you want to do it is fine with me."

I was counting on the fact that he wanted us to continue

72

to be a family even though Jeb was in prison. And I was right. Yet he didn't make me stronger. He made the way easier.

Lying there on the cool concrete, a feeling of peace came over me. There was no reason to hurry. It wouldn't be dark for hours. My head was clear and I felt relaxed. The children noticed the difference in me immediately. They had been too frightened by our near accident to say anything. They just kept looking at me cautiously, and I know they were wondering whether I was all right. Now they smiled as we got back into the car, and as I started the motor, they began to roughhouse and giggle. That was one of our favorite ways of breaking up the monotony of the drive.

We took our time and arrived home safely in the early evening. But never again would I make the trip in one day. We would stay at a motel if we had to, for as long as we could afford it.

I didn't know it then, but God was already working to solve the problem of our accommodations. We were about to become part of a story that began many years ago.

During World War II when London was being bombed day and night, the children in that city were evacuated. Some were sent to the countryside and some were sent to the United States. Usually there wasn't time for anyone to arrange for families to take the children in. The people in charge of the evacuation just did the best they could once they got the children to safety.

In Muncy, Pennsylvania, a middle-aged couple named Brock read an article in their newspaper about a shipload of 1,500 English children who were on their way to the United States, with no one but the crew to care for them. The Brocks were wealthy and had no children of their own, so they got in touch with the British Embassy and offered to take thirty of the young evacuees. Shortly before the ship arrived, Mr. Brock became ill and died. His widow was too grief-stricken to deal with thirty small children, so she withdrew her request for them. But after a few months of healing, she told the Embassy she would take the largest family they had left. And that was how the four Barlow children came to Muncy, Pennsylvania. They were brought up there, and Mrs. Brock was like a mother to them.

The Barlow children grew up, got married, and went their own ways, as children do, but whenever possible they return to their home. They love the old house. Sheila Barlow married a Muncy man. Her brother, Malcolm Barlow, lives in Philadelphia but spends part of each summer in the Brock home.

During the Fourth of July weekend in the summer that Jeb went to prison, one of his former New York City clients, Bob Frank, decided to visit him at Allenwood. Bob knew Malcolm Barlow and remembered that he spent part of his summers in Muncy, which is close to Allenwood. He called Malcolm Barlow and asked him where he might stay overnight, and Malcolm Barlow invited him to stay at his home.

Bob Frank stayed for two days and visited Jeb both afternoons. The first day he brought Malcolm Barlow along with him. When the men were leaving, Malcolm Barlow said to Jeb, "Do you think your wife and children would like to stay with my sister? She lives in Muncy, too."

Jeb was amazed and grateful. Much as we tried to keep it from him, he knew the trip was a strain on us. He said yes.

The next time we came to visit Jeb, Malcolm Barlow's sister also came. She wanted to look us over—and, frankly, I wanted to look her over, too. It took me about two seconds to recognize Sheila Barlow O'Brien as a real blessing, and I said a silent prayer of thanks as we sat with her on the prison patio.

"Have you checked into your motel yet?" she asked.

"Yes," I said.

"Then let this be the last time you have to do that. And plan on having dinner with us tonight, please."

For the rest of that summer—for as long as Jeb was in

Allenwood—we found a haven, a place of peace and comfort and love with the O'Briens. We stayed in Sheila's lovely farm home where she and her husband took us in and cared for us much as she herself had been taken in when she was a child.

On Fridays, we would go directly to Allenwood to see Jeb. When we left him around 3:15 there was still plenty of time for the children to have a swim in the pool at the O'Brien farm. While they had some fun, Sheila took me to neighboring farms where I bought fresh fruits and vegetables, country-cured bacon, and eggs. The rules at Allenwood had been changed: now I was allowed to bring Jeb some food. I chose the best fresh fruit and vegetables I could find because they were sadly missing from the prison diet.

At night we had dinner with the O'Briens in their beautiful old dining room. Often they invited a few friends to join us, which was their way of telling us we had no reason to hide from people. On Saturday, we went to visit Jeb again. If we were allowed to go to church services with Jeb on Sunday—which wasn't always a certainty—we stayed another night.

There were no words I could find to tell these wonderful friends what their kindness meant to us. In so many big and little ways, they had made our prison visits easier. Jeb didn't have to worry so much about us—we weren't in a strange motel room or pushing too hard to get home in a hurry. We all were more relaxed during visiting hours. It was as if someone else were helping to carry our burden—which is exactly what was happening. In the warmth of the O'Brien home, we were accepted not as people to be pitied but as those who needed refreshment for the journey ahead, and that is what they gave us.

Ever since I had seen the drab hollow-eyed men standing in the mailroom, watching the visitors, the one thing I wanted was to keep Jeb from becoming another unvisited prisoner. I had made up my mind that we *had* to keep coming to see him, yet every week as I drove home I could understand why so many wives gave up. The prison system works against us so effectively that the loss of a man's family almost becomes part of his sentence.

Everything about the trip was exhausting. There were so many little things to do before we left—arrange for the animals to be fed and cared for, fill up the gas tank and have the oil checked, take along all kinds of clothes to suit any kind of weather we might meet, bring books and games to keep the children from getting restless, and there were always papers and mail for Jeb to go over. Then there was the long drive. Most exhausting of all—now that I can look back on it—was the visit itself. We never discussed it then, but I realize that we all tried to put up a good front because there really wasn't anything else we could do. We had to suppress our true feelings to spare each other—and ourselves—the pain of them. And that took its toll of our energy. I could read the strain on Jeb's face and he could read it on mine. The children were happy when they were with Jeb, but leaving was hard for them. Would there come a day, I wondered, when we would decide it was better not to go through it all? I told myself it would never happen, but I was no longer sure I could make my vow stick. Just before we met the O'Briens, we were reaching our limit. I had stopped believing I was superhuman. Someone else would have to decide whether it was possible to keep our family together.

"Isn't it amazing," Malcolm Barlow said one evening months later, "I really don't know your husband's client that well. We only met a few times, and briefly. Isn't it a coincidence that he called me up that day?"

I knew then that it wasn't really a coincidence. It was God.

8

THERE WERE MANY TIMES in our marriage when Jeb had to be away overnight, and sometimes for several nights. So I was used to being alone in the house with children. But now things were different.

The first night I was alone I was awakened by the telephone around 1 o'clock in the morning. I picked up the phone as quickly as I could, before it could wake the children, and said, "Hello." No one answered. All I could hear was heavy breathing. That was to happen many times during the next several months. I told myself I shouldn't be afraid. My doors and windows were locked and I had a large German Shepherd dog to protect us. Our next-door neighbors had told me to call them *anytime* if I needed them. Nevertheless I was afraid. The realization that there were people who wanted to frighten us made my skin crawl.

Fear was taking over more of my life. I had been afraid for our home when the press laid siege to it. Now I was afraid for my husband and children, and for myself. There was no use telling myself I was only imagining things. I had seen the evidence of evil. I had seen it wherever people stopped looking at other people as human beings—in the drive for success, in the White House, in the news media, in the prosecutors' offices, and in prison.

I saw it in children. Most of our children's friends were

supportive, but there were a few who taunted cruelly. Whit never told me about it, but I learned from one of his friends that an older boy at school made some nasty remarks about Jeb. Usually Whit has an even disposition and the good sense to avoid fights, but on that day, he turned on the bigger boy, grabbed him, and pushed him up against a wall. "Don't you ever say that about my father again!" he said. He had no more trouble after that.

When I was in the kitchen one day, I heard some children taunting Stuart in our backyard. "Your father's going to jail! Your father's going to jail!" they chanted. Stuart was too little to do anything but cry. The children doing the chanting were almost twice his age.

Our children were wonderful. They never complained. They seemed to want to make things as easy for me as they could. But every now and then I would come upon Tracy sitting in her room, crying softly, and when I asked her what was the matter she always said, "Nothing. It's okay."

Whitney immediately stepped into the role of the father of the house. Sometimes, in the evenings, when I couldn't keep the tears back and went to my bedroom, he straightened up the kitchen and saw that the other children got into bed.

I was concerned about Justin and Tracy because they kept their feelings to themselves, and it was more difficult for me to know what was going on inside them. Justin at his age had a very serious outlook on life, and my best clues to his emotions came from his paintings. Tracy was unhappy in her new school but didn't want to burden me with her problems. I found out about them when I asked her which of her classmates she wanted to invite to her birthday party and she said, "None." The year before, she had invited the whole class. I decided to look into the possibility of enrolling her somewhere else.

Even in his bewilderment over the absence of his father, Stuart was a joy. He was the only real child among us, and we needed his uncomplicated gestures of affection. One morning when I was feeling particularly depressed, I was sitting on the edge of my bed in tears. The older children had left for school, but I heard Stuart moving around the kitchen. A few minutes later, I thought I was alone in the house, but then my bedroom door opened and Stuart came in carrying a tray. He was moving as fast as he dared. He put the tray on the bed beside me, hugged me, and ran out of the room, hurrying outside to his carpool. On the tray were a cup and saucer, the cup filled with espresso, cream, sugar, and a tea bag! When I thought of him going from one kitchen cabinet to the other, gathering up the ingredients for anything I might possibly want, I began to smile. Then I laughed and the terrible depression left me. How could I *not* be cheered? My children's love was a beautiful gift from God.

Much as I loved the children, I did not like being the only parent in the house all the time. Now that I couldn't share the discipline with Jeb, I was beginning to hate the edge that came into my voice when I said something like: "This is the last time I'm going to tell you to go to bed." Not that I had to say such things often. Our children are considerate and very good. But still they are children. I didn't seem to have much time for the fun things or the moments of closeness. With four totally different personalities and routines, I had to settle for trying to help them live as normally as possible. It seemed to be the only way I could soften their ordeal.

Now that I had to pay the bills and get the car and the house repaired, I had an even greater appreciation of Jeb's abilities. He used to take care of those things with ease, whereas I had to work at them. I was late paying the mortgage a few times. Luckily our house wasn't old and didn't need much in the way of repairs, but whenever anything went wrong it seemed to take forever to get someone to fix it. Even here God stepped in to help us. Before Jeb went away, we had water in our basement every time it rained, but while he was in prison it remained absolutely dry!

Our social life had come to a standstill with Watergate.

We were dropped from the Green Book, and to many people, we were an embarrassment rather than a social asset. The phone, at long last, was quiet, except for a few calls from reporters who wanted to know "how we were getting on." I appreciated the fact that some of the press were sympathetic to us and wanted to do an honest interview, but I couldn't seem to make it clear to them that I didn't want *anything* written. Publicity, even the favorable kind, only added to our problems. Why was it so hard for these reporters to understand? They would have felt the same need for peace if they had been in my situation.

The friends who remained, and the new ones we had made, became especially dear to us. Most of them were Christians who, like Jesus, were not put off by the stigma of scandal. One woman took the time to write me a little note of encouragement every few weeks. Others invited us to dinner and offered to care for the children.

If I had had my own way I probably would have become a recluse. The shock of separation was wearing off, and I could feel the pain Lynn Caine had predicted. At night, I was too tired to go anywhere for dinner. I really didn't want to see anyone or do anything except take care of my children and visit my husband. Fortunately, I didn't have my way. God saw fit to keep me busy.

Ever since we had moved to Washington, I had worked for the Junior League. For a while, I took telephone calls at the City Hall Complaint Center, helping to cut government red tape for residents with problems. Then I was a tour guide at the National Gallery of Art. When our world began to come apart, I thought I might have to give up volunteer work because I didn't think I would have time for it. But in the spring of 1974, shortly before Jeb went to prison, I was asked to direct a new Junior League project called "Washington Ear." It was a radio program for the blind and physically handicapped which the League was sponsoring and helping to fund. For eighteen hours a day, seven days a week, over a closed-circuit radio band, newspapers, magazines, and books would be read. Our job was to staff the programs and get special receivers into the hands of blind and handicapped listeners in the Washington area.

I had researched the project when the League was considering it and was very enthusiastic about it. When the League voted to fund the radio service, they graciously stuck their necks out by asking me to head the program. Somehow, I decided, I would find the time to do it.

There were many times later on when I thought I must have been out of my mind to take on such a massive job. I hoped I wasn't being selfish, because I wanted to do the work well. Finally I became convinced that the job and I were good for each other. God knew what he was doing. He wanted me to be busy—and He wanted me to meet someone.

Dr. Margaret Rockwell is an amazing woman. About ten years before I met her, she had been a housewife with a husband and a small son. They lived in Maryland, in one of the Washington suburbs. Then Margaret Rockwell began to go blind. The shock was more than her husband could accept, and he left her and their son.

Margaret Rockwell's mother came to live with her and helped take care of the boy and the house. During the day, Margaret taught herself Braille, a system of writing far more difficult to learn than French or Spanish. At night, Margaret went to school. She already had a B.S., but she wanted to get an advanced degree so she could make her living as a social worker. She got her doctorate and then got a job. Somewhere in between, she learned to get around with the aid of a guide dog, although she didn't always use one. When she was familiar with an area, such as her home or her office, she could get around as well as anybody, and one would never know she was blind. She walked confidently, her arms at her sides, remembering that it was so many steps this way and so many that way to get where she wanted to go.

When Margaret's brother in Wisconsin began to work

with a group of people who were organizing radio programs for the blind, Margaret became very interested. That, she decided, was what Washington needed. So she got her facts together and began talking to people about Washington Ear. She was so persuasive that radio station WETA donated the use of a closed-circuit radio band, an extremely generous gift. The Junior League contributed volunteers and some of the funding, and several other organizations, along with the local governments, gave a total of $108,000 to get the program started.

There was a lot to do. Getting the special receivers designed, produced, and into the hands of the blind and handicapped was the most difficult part. Doctors and hospitals are not allowed to give out names and addresses of patients, so we tried to make the blind members of the community aware of our project through radio commercials and newspaper feature articles. Organizations serving the blind also helped to direct people to us. We also had to plan the programs and train people to read clearly, expressively, and for long periods of time. It was impossible to read a whole newspaper every day, so a reader had to be able to scan and pick out the relevant information. That took practice.

Working with Margaret Rockwell was a blessing to me. She had absolutely no pity for herself and certainly none for me. Quite the opposite. In five minutes, she could assign me days of work to be done within hours. At first, her instructions made me dizzy because she knew her subject so well and I did not. But she didn't wait for me to catch up. She simply assumed I could do marvelous things—and I found myself trying to live up to her expectations. I had to grow—right in the midst of wanting to shrivel up. I couldn't excuse myself by saying, "You don't know how hard it is," because she did—even more than I.

I had grown up in a home where learning was exciting, fun. And I've never lost my appetite for knowledge. It felt good to stretch my mind and find ways to make Washington Ear work. Problems became challenges, and each time I met one, I became more confident. For a long time, I had been increasingly aware of my weaknesses. Now I was discovering my strengths.

One day I had a call from a friend who was going into the hospital for surgery on her eye. The retina had become detached and there was a chance it could be reattached by surgery. For several days after the six-hour operation she would have to lie absolutely still in a darkened room, with bandages over her eyes. She would have pain, but it was critically important that she must not move.

I gave her one of the closed-circuit receivers when I visited her in the hospital the day after surgery. A few weeks later my friend called to tell me how much Washington Ear had meant to her. "I couldn't have made it through that darkness without it," she said. "It kept me in touch with the world." If it meant that much to her, what must it mean to someone who is permanently blind?

There was another advantage in working with Dr. Rockwell. She was a trained social worker and she, better than many others, could understand my inner agony. She knew that underneath my calm exterior, I was terrified and lonely. She accepted my fears that something might happen to Jeb in prison. She sensed my concern that this trauma might affect our children for the rest of their lives. Just because I sounded cheerful, she didn't assume that everything was all right.

That was one of the problems I had with the press. When I refused to give interviews, some reporters wrote about me anyway. Unable to quote me, they characterized me. I was "the well-dressed, well-coiffed young matron" who seemed to be getting along just fine, even though her husband was in prison. Our children were always "well-behaved" and "good-looking," apparently unmarked by the loss of their father. Didn't they know? Couldn't they look beneath the surface? Or did they think that only people with mussed clothing and uncombed hair could get hurt?

If I had lost friends, I had also gained some. I was in charge of forty-five volunteers, and I tried to get to know each one personally. It was a wonderful new area of relationships where I could start from scratch. At least there, the White House didn't matter anymore. Neither did Watergate. We had a job to do.

I was touched by God's incredible kindness. He seemed to think of everything. Here were all these new personal contacts at the very time when my covenant group stopped meeting for the summer. He knew I was not strong enough to keep myself going.

Jeb and I wrote to each other every night. Our letters were very different from any we had ever written before. I gave Jeb news of the children and my work, and then I would add some notes from my Bible Study Fellowship course. Jeb had hardly any news for me, but he was in a Yokefellows covenant group and was also studying the Bible. He used to read his Bible every night and then write to me before going to sleep. It helped him to think more clearly about what he had read if he put his thoughts into words. And his words helped me. There was so much we had to learn, so much we had never known.

We were becoming aware of the Holy Spirit. At first, when Louie Evans explained it to us, we found it difficult to believe that Jesus Christ actually lived within each of us. We could believe it of some other people we knew. They seemed to be directed by an inner voice. But if that voice was in us why hadn't it spoken up sooner? Why hadn't it warned us about what was happening to our lives?

Then, again, the veil was lifted a little more. There *had* been warning signals. All those vague doubts I used to have about the men on the White House Staff—my fear of Chuck

Colson, my distrust of John Dean, my aversion to Bob Haldeman—were not the imaginings of a wife who didn't know what she was talking about. They were the rib-poking messages of the Holy Spirit within me. He had given me the gift of sensitivity and insight into other people. The only problem was, I didn't know it. Long before I even realized there was such a thing as the Holy Spirit, his voice was in me. I didn't hear it because I wasn't listening.

Like everyone else, Jeb and I were born with an instinctive knowledge of good and evil. Yet we constantly chose evil over good. It seemed to be the way of the world. All around us we saw people drinking too much, polluting themselves just as they also polluted the earth with their excesses. We saw them trying to escape from their responsibilities to each other. Success and ambition came before love. We were no different. We didn't know there *was* anything different. The voice that whispered warnings seemed to be just an old-fashioned concept called "conscience" that could be explained away.

In a way, Jeb and I were lucky. It took a crisis to do it, but our priorities had been shattered, and now they had to be rearranged. We had to learn a whole new way to live. We had asked for help and Christ had come into our lives. But that was only the beginning. Giving him control over our decisions, our behavior, and our goals was going to be very difficult for us both. Much as we knew that we couldn't trust our own sense of direction, we were in the habit of doing things for ourselves. It would be a long time before we could change.

We wondered how we could be sure it was the Holy Spirit speaking to us. There were other voices—our own, our friends'. How could we tell the difference?

Gradually, as each of us learned what it meant to study God's Word, the answer became apparent. The more we knew about Jesus Christ, the more we would recognize his voice among all the others. That's why it was so important for us to understand what the Bible was all about.

At night, when I wrote to my husband, I found myself knowing that something good would come out of the wreckage of our lives. I couldn't be sure whether that was wishful thinking on my part—or the work of the Spirit. But I knew that someday in the future I would be able to say, "Praise the Lord!" for what had happened.

9

AT ALLENWOOD, I FOUND I had advantages some other wives did not have and that bothered me. I was white, I was educated, and I wasn't intimidated by a bureaucratic employee. There were very few other visitors in my situation.

The first few times the children and I visited Jeb, the guards looked at everything in my shopping bag. Later, when they began to recognize me, they just took a peek and let it go at that. But many of the other visitors had to go through the same routine no matter how many times they came—everything in every package had to be checked, and not always quickly.

The guards were courteous but arbitrary. Sometimes, when they were supposed to call an inmate's dormitory and tell him he had visitors, they didn't, and I saw several sad, bewildered wives sitting in the reception room for hours, wondering why their husbands never showed up. I could imagine the anxiety their husbands must have suffered—did they picture their wives lying dead on the road somewhere, victims of an accident? Or did they think their wives had decided not to come anymore? It was a cruel form of harassment, and there wasn't anything a visitor could do about it. Complain, and you were told you could leave if you didn't like the way things were.

Many of the inmates at Allenwood were black or Puerto

Rican, uneducated, and poor. This is true of prisons in general. It is misleading to think of these inmates as underprivileged because someone surely will say, "Well, they have the same rights as the rest of us—why don't they do something about their lives?" Theoretically they do have the same rights as the rest of us—but they don't know how to use them. Nor is anyone about to teach them.

Working at the City Hall Complaint Center in Washington had given me my first close contact with the poor. We used to get calls from mothers whose children had been bitten by rats or whose landlords found ways to avoid repairing plumbing fixtures that leaked raw sewage from one apartment to another. Our telephone number was always printed on the front page of the daily newspaper, next to the numbers for the police and fire departments, yet we were always their last resort. First they would go to their landlords, who usually put them off with the excuse that "someone would be around to look at the place in about ten days." When no one ever came, the tenants went back to the landlord a second and perhaps a third time. Then they went to the Board of Health. Still, nothing happened. More children were bitten by rats, and sewage continued to run down the walls. Finally, probably because they heard about the Complaint Center from someone they knew, they came to us—not in anger, but in resignation. They expected another putdown. How different they were from the well-to-do residents in Northwest Washington who could become absolutely irate if their garbage wasn't picked up on time!

The poor didn't know that they didn't have to live in conditions of filth and hazard. They didn't know that, when a landlord made excuses, they didn't have to accept them. They didn't know how to talk back to the bureaucratic voice at the Board of Health when it expressed surprise that no one had come "to investigate the premises." When the poor came to us, we simply made use of the rights they didn't know they had—and that's how red tape gets cut. We—in our "cultured" voices—got a totally different response from a landlord. Usually he made the necessary repairs. If we called the Board of Health, we had no patience with any details about how busy they were. We demanded action and we usually got it.

The work was depressing. For each person we helped, we knew there were thousands of others who didn't even realize that any kind of aid was available. We wondered how anyone could say that their opportunities were equal to ours when we knew about such things and they didn't.

In Washington, the poor had been voices at the other end of a telephone. In Allenwood, I saw their faces. If they didn't know they had rights when they were on the outside, how could they possibly know they had rights in prison?

Jeb's sentence was unusual in that he was given a minimum and a maximum amount of time to serve. Technically he would become eligible for parole upon serving the minimum amount of time, although we were to learn that paroles are almost never granted that early. Most of the inmates in Allenwood were serving indeterminate sentences, meaning that they could not be imprisoned *longer* than a certain amount of time. They became eligible for parole upon serving one third of their maximum sentence—i.e., a man sentenced to prison for up to fifteen years could apply for parole after serving five years.

Like Jeb and me, most people think parole is automatic once a prisoner becomes eligible for it. Quite the opposite is true. Eligibility doesn't mean much because most parole boards deny a prisoner's application the first time around. The board members don't know anymore about an inmate than they can glean from a bureaucratic file. They know nothing about his family situation or the kind of life that awaits him outside prison. They usually have their minds made up before they interview the prisoner: parole denied, no explanation necessary. How else could so many prisoners—even model inmates—fail to meet their criteria?

When a man is denied parole, he is, in reality, being sentenced all over again. Before he becomes eligible again he has to serve whatever period of time the parole board may set. He hopes that nothing goes wrong and that he won't get involved in anything that will spoil his record for good behavior—because eventually, that good behavior is the only thing that will get him out of prison without serving the full maximum sentence.

Some prisoners had lawyers to advise them before they began serving their sentence, but once they are in prison, their lawyers lose interest in them. Few have anyone to help them with their problems. If their family is being evicted or if someone is ill, there is no one to whom they can turn for advice. In the entire prison at Allenwood, there were only three social workers.

Bill Edwards was an example. He was young—only twenty-seven—and had been at Allenwood for almost three years. One day he got a letter from his former wife who had divorced him and married another man. She and their young son had been badly beaten by her new husband. The boy's leg was broken. Could Bill do anything to get the boy out of danger until she had a chance to straighten out her life?

Bill almost went mad with frustration. There was no way he could get to his son—an emergency furlough was denied. And the social worker said he couldn't do a thing to help. Bill had a sister in Virginia, but she said she couldn't take care of the boy because she went to work every day.

Somehow Bill managed to borrow enough money to bring the boy east from California. Then his sister reluctantly agreed to meet the boy at the airport—and nothing more. I don't know what would have happened to him if Sue Krogh hadn't offered to take care of him for a few weeks. Sue understood how things were. Her husband, Egil, had served 4 months at Allenwood just before Jeb went in.

I knew about Bill because, like many of the inmates, he thought Jeb could help him solve his problems. From the other prisoners' point of view, Jeb was in a position of power —he was white, educated, and had been in the White House. Some of them seemed to think he was still in the White House and could help them get a parole or a reduced sentence. The way they looked at it, only the poor and the powerless ended up in prison, and they were confused by Jeb's presence among them. They didn't always believe him when he said he had absolutely no influence in the government anymore. But he did try to help some of the prisoners with their parole applications. He understood red tape and the often meaning-less procedures of a bureaucracy—and a prison, after all, is just that. In that sense, Jeb was better prepared for prison than many of the others. He had had experience with bigness, both in the corporate world and in the government. He wasn't shocked when the system didn't work; he didn't expect it to, and he had an amazing amount of patience with people who didn't seem to know what they were doing. Some of the younger prisoners who had never had a chance to get out and work in the world were so shocked by the sudden realization that they didn't matter to anyone in the system that they broke down. Jeb was hurt by it, but he had seen it before.

Jeb had other problems, one of which was time. There isn't much for a man to do in prison, and Jeb is a person who likes to work and think and create. For a while he was assigned to kitchen duty, and then later, he was given some clerical work to do, but only for a few hours a day. The rest of the time he could lie on his bunk—as many inmates did— or sit in a chair, or take a short walk. Most of the beautiful prison grounds were off limits to the inmates. There were two tennis courts which the prison authorities boasted about, but they were in bad condition. Jeb had me buy about $100 worth of tape and nails so he could repair them and teach some of the inmates to play.

Jeb read a lot. Every week I brought him more books. So did almost everyone who visited him. He had several versions of the Bible and was comparing them as he read. Then, one day, he asked me to bring him a set of paints. I was in such a hurry to answer his request that I made a mistake. I bought him a box of watercolors, the most difficult medium in which to work, and Jeb was just a beginner. He did the best he could with them, but I could see he wasn't achieving enough to get any satisfaction out of painting. He was rescued by our good friend, Gene Arnold, who brought him a set of oils. Jeb was able to do much better with them and really seemed to be developing a feeling for art.

For the first time in his life, Jeb was forced to slow down the pace of his life. It wasn't comfortable, but it gave him an opportunity to realize that he didn't have to spend every single moment doing something practical. He may have started painting out of boredom, but it touched something in him. He was discovering that he had a capacity to appreciate loveliness, creativity, and interpretation—nor were they simply ornaments in his life. They spoke to his mind and his spirit, and he found he could express his thoughts in new ways. I began to hope these things would become so important to him that he would never again exclude them from his life. But there was no way of knowing what the future would bring.

When some of the rules were relaxed and visitors could bring food to the inmates, I used to arrive with a bagful of fresh raspberries, peaches, grapes, plums, tomatoes, and anything else I could find in that lush farming area. Jeb loved seeing them, but he couldn't eat them. He didn't have any appetite. He had begun to lose weight. He lost over 20 pounds in those early months of prison. Usually the children finished the fruit.

We weren't allowed to bring in anything to drink because the authorities wanted to keep liquor from the inmates. They didn't succeed. We occasionally saw empty liquor bottles in the trash cans! Some people weren't even going to the trouble of using less incriminating containers. Somehow that was symbolic of the depression that was so prevalent in prison. It was as if the inmates were asking to be caught—because that was the only way they could get any attention positive or negative.

Little by little, Jeb was learning the ways of prison life. I noticed that his uniforms were pressed, and one day an inmate came up to us and said, "Hey, Jeb, how did your wife like the uniform?"

"Just fine," Jeb said.

When the man left, Jeb told me that he worked in the prison laundry and would press a man's uniform in exchange for one or two packs of cigarettes. (He could also get even with someone by burning his clothes!) That explained why Jeb, who didn't smoke, had been buying cigarettes at the prison commissary. Since the prisoners weren't allowed to have any money, the barter system was their only means of purchasing power.

I was allowed to go to church with Jeb on Sunday morning more often, and soon it became something I could count on. It was a strange experience, so different from the joy and warmth of our home church. The church was on the prison grounds, about a half mile from the administration building, which was as far as prisoners were allowed to walk. Only about eight or ten inmates attended the Protestant services, and, instead of sitting together in an attitude of fellowship, each man seemed to sit as far away from any other as he possibly could. Most of the time we had a minister, although not always the same one, and a woman played the piano so we could sing some hymns. But it was a sad, uninspired gathering. God was there, but his presence was not celebrated.

According to the rules, wives and children of inmates could stay on after church only if there weren't a lot of other visitors. On Sunday, however, especially in the summer, there always were a lot of visitors. None of the guards ever told me we couldn't stay, but I saw them deny the privilege to some of the other wives, particularly the young wives of the draft evaders. Our family was large and theirs were small, only one or two, so it didn't make sense to let us in and keep them out. It was clearly a form of harassment. I was grateful to be able to worship with Jeb, but the discrimination made me angry.

There were two days a year when the prisoners were allowed to enjoy the prison grounds beyond the administration building. The Yokefellows sponsored a picnic in July and the Jaycees sponsored one in August. They were the most exciting events of the entire year, and many prisoners who didn't participate in the Yokefellows' or Jaycees' programs volunteered to cook or clean up just to share in the good times.

And they were good times, considering the circumstances. From the moment the visitors began to arrive, it was evident that the prisoners' families had gone to a lot of trouble to make the event special.

There are different social levels at Allenwood, just as there are in other parts of our society, and they were especially evident at the picnics. The poor arrived in broken-down cars and ate simple sandwiches, sitting on the ground or on rocks. The OC—organized crime—visitors came in big, expensive cars, ready to prepare a sumptuous feast. The steaks they barbecued were the biggest I had ever seen, and each man was given a whole one.

Among the less typical visitors were the wives and children of two brothers who were serving sentences at the same time because the company they owned had been involved in fraudulent practices. The families pulled up in two station wagons piled high with food and equipment. They brought their own barbecues and tables, and they sat on some very good-looking deck chairs. The women wore well-cut pantsuits and their husbands, the inmates, were in their tennis clothes. In spite of the sweltering heat, they managed to look cool. The women had brought along about thirty filet mignons and thirty lobster tails which they barbecued and served to their husbands and their inmate friends.

A lot of children came to the picnics and the inmates had scheduled an active day for them. One of the inmates was Johnny Sample, the former professional football player. He was in charge of the sports program, which included running races and tugs-of-war. Whitney and Justin were away at camp by that time, so only Tracy and Stuart were with us. They had a marvelous time and won two trophies each. They also enjoyed the free ice cream and Coke supplied by the Yokefellows all day long.

It was so good to be able to move around and not be confined to the reception room and the patio. The grounds were lovely and we took short walks by the lake near the woods. The children were amazing. They seemed to sense our need to be together. Now that they were more familiar with the visiting routine and knew some of the other children who came to Allenwood, they would leave us from time to time so that we could be alone.

There was one unhappy aftermath of the summer picnics. Visitors and inmates had been told that three things were forbidden—drugs, drinking, and sex. But some of the inmates did get together with their wives or girlfriends and they mentioned it in their letters, perhaps for the same reason they threw liquor bottles in the trash cans: to cry out for attention. They were immediately removed to Lewisburg penitentiary. By law, prisoners' mail cannot be read—although it can be checked for contraband—but the law isn't obeyed in prison and there isn't anything an inmate can do about it.

We were glad the press didn't know about the picnics, because surely they would have revived the image of the "country club prison." They had followed Jeb to Allenwood,

and for the first few weeks he was there he found himself
dodging them as much as he had at home. When he went in,
he asked to be spared any interviews by the press, but the
prison authorities were flattered by the sudden attention they
were getting from the news media. If someone called up and
said he wanted to do a story on Allenwood because he heard
it was a fine example of a penal institution, he usually got
in. And once he got in, he could get to Jeb.

One day in June, Jeb was making his bed when the
warden came into the dormitory, leading a group of reporters on a so-called tour of the prison. When they spotted Jeb,
they immediately came over and began to ask him a lot of
questions. Without Jeb's knowledge or permission, one of
the reporters copied down the words of a Father's Day poem
Whit had written for Jeb. It was lying on Jeb's desk. The
next day it appeared in *The New York Times*, much to our
horror. I don't know whether the reporter even considered
that he was invading the privacy of a father and his son, but
they were hurt by the exposure. Whit felt betrayed by the
publication of his innermost feelings, which he had confided
only to Jeb—and Jeb felt helplessly furious because he was
unable to do anything about it. Some of our friends were
puzzled when they read the newspaper and called to ask me
why we would allow such a private expression to be printed.
They didn't know (and neither did we, until then) that such
things could happen.

One Saturday when we were visiting Jeb outside on the
crowded patio, I looked past Jeb's shoulder and thought I
was seeing things. There in the window of the warden's
office—and aimed straight at us—was a TV camera. We
could just imagine the commentary that would accompany
the film—"Jeb Magruder and family enjoying a lovely Saturday afternoon at their country club prison." Someone had
talked the warden into allowing him to do a documentary
on prison life, but, as the cameraman began to stalk us, it was

only too obvious whose life they were after. For the rest of the visiting hours we ducked back and forth from patio to reception room.

There is no such thing as a country club prison. The only distinction that can be made among prisons in general is that some are worse than others, not better. Cells can be worse than dormitories and armed guards are more threatening than unarmed guards. But the real horror of prison—*any* prison —is its systematic dehumanization of a person. A prisoner is not even an animal. He is a thing.

I used to worry about Jeb's safety, even in that country club prison. Violent emotions ran very close to the surface in most prisoners. They knew they were impotent, and it filled them with rage. Jeb never wanted to talk about it, but I heard stories of fights and brutal beatings. Suddenly one prisoner would be marked for retaliation and no one knew why. Jeb got along well with everyone—he always had—but I was afraid that even his remarkable disposition might work against him. To many of the poor in prison, Jeb was a lucky man. He had a family, he was trained to do a job, he knew how to handle himself in a lot of situations. Perhaps, one day, these things would be reason enough to someone to strike out at him.

Jeb was unusual in another way. He admitted his guilt. Most prisoners couldn't. At first it seemed like a joke, hearing man after man declare his innocence—except that there was nothing laughable about it. Then I began to understand. These men weren't saying they didn't do something wrong. They were saying they had done the same thing they saw lots of other people doing and getting away with.

At Allenwood, only a handful of prisoners were serving time for crimes of violence. Most of them were sentenced for drug use, theft, and burglary, plus a few for income tax evasion, Medicare fraud, and, in Jeb's case, conspiracy to obstruct justice. So they weren't claiming that everyone else

D

was violent. They were claiming that everyone else was as dishonest as they were, and they were bitter about the fact that they were being punished for their crimes while others went free. Perhaps their point of view was exaggerated and it may have been colored by rationalizations—but there also was a basis of truth in it.

I felt that Jeb had assumed far more than his share of guilt for Watergate and some of the other illegal campaign practices. In fact, I couldn't finish reading his book because I thought he was too hard on himself. I also saw that, even though he accepted his sentence as a penalty for the things he had done, the experience of prison was not alleviating his guilt. If anything, it seemed to grow every time he saw us, and I knew it was because he felt responsible for our pain. If he saw that we were able to handle a situation, he was relieved—but at the same time, he felt helpless because we were doing it without him. I couldn't expect him to react differently. I had to accept it as part of his prison sentence and hope it would end when the sentence did.

But when would it end? We had prepared ourselves for 10 months, thinking he would have to serve only the minimum part of his sentence. Once Jeb was in prison, he learned what most lawyers and judges don't seem to know—that parole boards rarely let a prisoner serve only the minimum part of his sentence. Usually they deny parole until *at least* a third to a half of the maximum sentence has been served. That meant Jeb wouldn't be out for at least sixteen months—and perhaps more. Even with good behavior, parole is not automatic.

So now there was no end in sight. Prison and separation stretched ahead of us indefinitely. I knew I would have to begin facing some new problems. If we didn't have enough money to last until Jeb was released, that would be especially hard on the children, and they were the ones I wanted to protect. We would have to move away from their friends and take them out of their schools. I would have to get a job —which I wouldn't have minded, except for the fact that I wanted to be available to the children whenever they needed me. That was especially important now that I was the only parent at home.

Jeb, in his practical, farsighted way, tried to get me to come to grips with these problems as we sat on the prison patio each weekend. But I still had my mind set on ten months and I couldn't accept anything longer. Somewhere inside myself I knew I would have to, eventually. I just wasn't ready yet. I wasn't trying to escape from all of reality—only part of it. I could handle only so much of it at a time.

10

AT LEAST, in those hot summer months, we could sit outdoors. We wondered what it would be like in winter with all of us crowded into the reception room. Sometimes the roads would be icy and we always would be worrying about a snowstorm. But God was going to lead us around those problems—although by a harrowing route.

The Watergate trial was scheduled to begin in October, and the prosecutors wanted to prepare their witnesses. At the end of July, they summoned Jeb back to Washington for a day. This time he was put in handcuffs and was escorted by two federal marshals. Instead of traveling by car, which would have taken four hours, they flew, and from a little town like Allenwood that was a complicated procedure. They left Allenwood at 5 o'clock in the morning and arrived in Washington six hours later. Jeb spent the rest of the day at the prosecutors' offices, undergoing the same kind of interrogation he had been given before he went into prison. There was one major difference: he was a prisoner now, and if anything, he was even less of a human being in their eyes.

At the end of the day, he was told he would be taken to the county jail for the night. Jeb had heard that Herbert Kalmbach and Charles Colson were at Fort Holabird in Baltimore and he asked whether he could be sent there. Jill Vollner, the prosecutor working with him, said there was no more room at Holabird. The county jail would have to do.

Jeb was allowed to call me before he left the prosecutors' offices, but there wasn't much he could say. He didn't know anything about the county jail or its visiting regulations, so we couldn't arrange to see each other. He thought it might be better for us to meet at Jill Vollner's office, although she wasn't receptive to the idea.

At 10 o'clock the next morning, Jeb called again. He sounded strange. Then suddenly I couldn't understand what he was saying. He was hysterical. Something terrible had happened to him.

When he had been taken to the county jail, he was given nothing to eat. He couldn't have eaten, anyway, not after what he saw. The county jail was a series of cells about 4 feet by 6 feet. Two men occupied each cell. They slept in bunk beds that were too small for the average man, and Jeb is six foot two. A man couldn't sit up in the lower bunk because his head hit the upper bunk. If he tried to sit on the upper bunk, his head hit the ceiling. At the end of the beds, and right up against them, was an open toilet. There was a sink—nothing else.

Jeb's clothes were taken away and he was given worn, unlaundered prison clothes. A cold shower was available, after which Jeb had to put on the same dirty clothes again. It was impossible to sleep because the lights were not turned off. A television set in the hall outside the cells was on all night. Men moaned and cried and argued and cursed and threatened and pleaded in their dreams. It was crowded, dirty, and stiflingly hot. Some men had been there for fifteen months, awaiting trial.

Jeb knew he was there for only one night. The next day he would be going back to Allenwood—and by comparison Allenwood looked very good. But the awareness of so many other men, not only in Washington, but in jails and prisons all over the country, stunned him. They couldn't get out. The brutality of their minute-by-minute existence was more than his mind could accept all at once. Slowly, gradually, their suffering ate away at his sensitivity through the long, sleepless night.

In the morning, Jeb was given a razor to shave himself, but he had to use cold water. His own clothes were returned to him so he could make himself presentable for the prosecutors.

When he got to the prosecutors, he called me—and that's when he broke down. While he was talking to me, Jill Vollner walked into the room and I was afraid to imagine how he must have looked when she saw him. "I'm sorry—" I heard him say, "I think I scared Jill Vollner."

It was so terrible to hear him that way, to know he was in pain and not be able to reach out and touch him or put my arms around him. For his sake, I didn't want to cry, but I couldn't help it.

Jill Vollner *was* scared. Neither she nor the other prosecutors were trying to abuse Jeb by sending him to the county jail. They just didn't seem to think—nor did they know—what the county jail was like. When they saw what one night had done to one of their star witnesses, they were horrified. Jeb would be of no value to them in this condition.

Jeb was returned to Allenwood the next day. Later, when the prosecutors sent for him again, suddenly there was room for him at Fort Holabird. He was transferred there on August 24.

Jeb had been granted a furlough the weekend he was to be transferred. I couldn't imagine how wonderful it would be to have him home again, and then I realized that we would be besieged by the press. So we made other plans. The O'Briens offered us the Brock home for the weekend, which was just perfect. The children were so excited, knowing they would be able to wake up and find their father with them. All week long friends kept stopping by, bringing us gifts of food.

On Thursday night, the phone rang and it was Jeb. I wasn't expecting to hear from him, and I knew immediately that there would be no furlough. He didn't even have to say it. The Allenwood warden, who had originally granted his permission for the furlough, had changed his mind. Since Jeb was now at Holabird, he would have had to be returned to the Allenwood jurisdiction before beginning his furlough. I had planned to pick him up there. But the marshals at Holabird said that their duties did not include transporting a prisoner from a Department of Justice jurisdiction (Holabird) to a Federal Bureau of Prisons jurisdiction (Allenwood).

I didn't know what to do, and I dreaded telling the children. They had spent the day packing our car full of food, clothes, and sports equipment. It was too cruel a disappointment. So I called Jill Vollner and asked her what happened. I don't know what I expected from her, but the coldness of her attitude was like a slap in my face. She said she didn't know anything about the furlough cancelation, but she would find out what happened and call me the next morning. She never called.

The next day the children and I cried as we unpacked our things and put away the suitcases. But at least we had each other. Jeb had to take the disappointment alone. At that moment, the knowledge that Jeb was being transferred to a prison closer to home was a very small consolation.

One of the passages we had been studying in my Bible Study Fellowship course came back to me. Paul said, "Don't worry so much about tomorrow—don't borrow trouble." I had understood it when we studied it, but now I realized how it fitted into my life. We had been worried about getting through the winter at Allenwood—as if there had been anything we could do about it. Again, we had fallen into our old habit of shifting for ourselves—or trying to—and not doing a very good job of it. We had prayed for help, thinking it would come as some form of an ability to endure. But that was like specifying the way we wanted our prayers answered.

Had we been deaf to the voice of the Holy Spirit? Didn't

the voice tell us all along that there *would* be help? That we could count on it? Shouldn't we have prayed in thanksgiving, knowing that God would take care of tomorrow—and the next day, and the day after that? I was learning more about what it meant to be a Christian. You didn't stop feeling—in fact, you became more sensitive to the hurts in life. You still had plenty of problems and you were concerned about them. But you didn't *worry*. You never had to wonder whether you would get through a difficult situation. You gave all that anxiety over to Jesus, because he was strong enough to carry it and you weren't. There really was such a thing as going through a crisis with a relaxed attitude. I hadn't achieved that yet, but I believed in it. I had seen it in others.

Some people might say that God did a terrible thing to Jeb by leading him out of Allenwood by way of the county jail. It was terrible but there was a purpose in it. Jeb broke down partly because of his own experience of humiliation and fear, and partly because of his abrupt awareness of so much human suffering. There was no other way he could have known about such things, and they changed his life. He had always been a considerate, warm, open person, but now there was a new dimension to his sensitivity. He felt the hurts of other people, and he felt them deeply.

In the sheltered world where Jeb and I had spent our lives up to that point, we came across different kinds of problems from those one finds in prisons. There is trauma and there is pain, but very seldom is there absolute helplessness to do anything about them. In our former world, people weren't isolated, locked away from contact with other free human beings, and impressed daily with the fact that they had been rejected by the rest of society. It is devastating to feel that no one cares about you—and I say this as someone who observed it from the outside. I only visited prison. I didn't live there. Jeb did. And even though God made it possible for the children and me to let him know we cared, he understood the agony of men who no longer believed they mattered. Even more than understanding it, he wanted to do something about it.

Holabird had lessons for both of us, and I am convinced that was one of the reasons why Jeb was sent there.

Fort Holabird itself was not a prison. It was an old army base that was being phased out. Temporarily, the federal government was using some of the facilities as a "safe house" for prisoners whose lives would have been endangered in a traditional prison. Except for the four Watergate witnesses who were housed there as a convenience, the fourteen other inmates were mostly Mafia hit men and members of several international drug-smuggling rings. In exchange for lighter sentences and the promise of new identities, these men had given information against their former associates, and for that, they were marked for death.

The soldiers were gone from Holabird. The gates and doors and prisoners were now guarded by federal marshals, all of them armed. A fifteen-foot-high wire fence enclosed the entire section surrounding the safe house, which was a former officers' barracks. At the gate and at the door to the safe house, my identification was carefully checked each time I entered. These guards were not at all like those at Allenwood. They were taking no chances. Their job was to keep the prisoners in, keep them from killing each other, and keep them from being killed by persons from the outside. Understandably, they were tense.

Each prisoner had a room to himself and shared a bath with another inmate. Jeb's room was 9 by 9 feet square and included a privilege we had not known for some time—a door. We all welcomed the privacy.

Holabird was only an hour away from our home, a happy change from the four-hour drive to Allenwood. Now that I didn't have to drive with my eyes riveted on the road, I could have a decent conversation with my children. If one of them had a problem, that was a good time for us to talk about it.

Visiting hours were from 3 to 6 P.M. three days a week and from 1 to 6 P.M. Saturdays and Sundays. Usually we went there on weekends, although several times I also went on Wednesdays. If I went on a weekday, I didn't take the children with me because that would have meant taking them out of school, which I didn't think was a good idea. I didn't like leaving them alone for those few hours after school until I came home, but usually I had no choice. I had already taken advantage of my friends' and neighbors' generosity in caring for the children and just couldn't bring myself to ask more of them. Many other people were always saying, "Why don't you leave the children with us sometime?" but they never got down to specifics and asked, "When can I look after the children?" I wasn't worried about how our children would behave at home alone—they never had given me a reason to worry. I was more concerned about the possibility of fires and accidents, which I somehow felt I could prevent if I were home with them. My mother feelings run very strong.

The four Watergate witnesses had been told to avoid talking to each other as much as possible until after the trial, so we didn't see much of Herb Kalmbach, John Dean, and Chuck Colson in the beginning. Sometimes, when I arrived at the safe house, I noticed Herb Kalmbach using the phone in the hall—the only one available to the prisoners. He often looked terrible. He was thin and pale and very sad. He allowed no visitors, even though his wife wanted to move to Baltimore to be near him. He insisted she remain in California, where they had a home and friends. He wanted to shield her as much as possible from the agony of his experience. A few times, when I saw him talking on the phone, he was crying, and I assumed he was talking to his wife.

I liked Herb. He was a gracious, gentle person, even in the midst of this depressing environment. We often talked together in the tiny kitchen or the dining room. He was always courteous and concerned about our family. He and Jeb tried to run 3 to 5 miles a day, and the physical self-discipline helped to keep their spirits at a reasonable level. I was glad, too, to learn that Herb was reading his Bible every day, because I knew what it meant to Jeb and me.

Chuck Colson, we learned, had experienced a conversion. He was visited often by Senator Harold Hughes and Doug Coe of the Christian Fellowship Foundation. His wife, Patti, who is a lovely, kind woman, was there every visiting day.

John Dean was hardly ever at Holabird. We never knew the details of his arrangement with the prosecutors, but it became obvious that he had obtained some concessions, mostly in the nature of conveniences. Before being assigned to Holabird, John had not been in prison at all. When he was at Holabird, he spent six days a week at the prosecutors' offices, where he was given a small office of his own and access to a telephone. He was only at Holabird at night and sometimes on Sundays, where he had a special armed guard twenty-four hours a day at his door. Sometimes on Sundays, I used to see his former wife—who was a neighbor of mine—arriving with their son to visit him. We saw his wife Maureen a few times. She was an attractive, stylishly dressed woman—and very frightened. She would come in the front door and run—literally run—down the hall and up the stairs to John's room, never looking right or left. On her way out, she did the same thing.

I could understand how she felt. There was a lot to fear at Holabird. It was frightening to see other prisoners, knowing why they were there. One man had killed twenty-seven people, another thirty. It was a long time before my mind could even accept those facts. It was frightening to see the federal marshals with their guns tucked into their belts. I had never been in the presence of so much potential brutality.

I began to be afraid for Jeb. The inmates of the safe

house were allowed to come and go as they pleased in the building, so unless Jeb stayed in his room, as John Dean did, he would have to mingle with them. How would men like that react to him? He was an outsider. Suppose they decided to kill him? After all, why not? What did one more death mean to them? And who would stop them? Suppose their hot tempers, which seemed always to be so near the surface, erupted and they fought among themselves? Would the guards shoot? Would they really care who got in the way of their bullets?

Because Holabird would soon be closed down, and since there were only eighteen prisoners and their guards, there was no kitchen staff. Each prisoner was paid $8 a day for his food, toiletries, and recreational needs, and it was up to him to take care of his own meals. I have no doubt that most of the men wouldn't have eaten well at all if it hadn't been for the organizational talents of the Mafia men among them. Even in prison, they had their leaders, lieutenants, and disciplined troops. Their leaders decided that each inmate should take his turn preparing meals for the others, which meant that each man was in charge of the kitchen every eighteenth day. It was that man's responsibility to plan the menu and see to it that a list of everything he needed was given in advance to those who did the marketing.

Once each week, two inmates escorted by two guards went out to buy food. The trip took most of the day because these men were not the kind who went to the local supermarket. They were very fussy about what they ate and they were accustomed to the best that money could buy. And with $8 a day for each man, they could continue eating the same way. It was their custom to go to many different shops—one for meat, another for poultry, another for vegetables and fruits, another for cheeses and cold cuts, and still another for the delectable Italian pastries that concluded most of their dinners. On Saturdays, they shopped again for fruits and vegetables.

At first, when I visited Holabird, I was allowed to eat with Jeb and the other inmates in the first-floor dining room, and I can attest that the food was on a gourmet level. It was delicious and beautifully prepared. Usually the man in charge of the kitchen spent his whole day cooking—it gave him something to do.

Boredom was even more of a problem at Holabird than it was at Allenwood. Here there were no jobs other than cooking every eighteenth day. Unless a man could amuse himself there was absolutely nothing for him to do. A lot of the men took heavy tranquilizers, such as Thorazine, so that they were either asleep or in a stupor most of the time. Jeb had his paints, and they helped. There was no Yokefellow covenant group at Holabird, but Louie Evans was able to visit Jeb occasionally. Jeb relied even more on my Bible Study Fellowship notes. It was so much easier for us to talk about the Bible now that we had a room to ourselves.

The children were delighted to be able to see more of their father. I was able to bring Katina, our dog, with us a few times. She is really Jeb's dog. He trained her when she was a puppy, and there is a special communication between them. The first time I brought her to Holabird she almost knocked him down with affection, and then the rest of the day she just stayed very close to him, her head on his lap. Now and then she made tiny whimpering sounds as if begging him not to send her away.

I knew it would be hard for four healthy active children to avoid becoming restless in a nine-by-nine-foot room for five hours, so I always came loaded down with books and games. Little by little, though, the children began to leave Jeb's room and explore the building. It was only natural for them to do that, but I found myself worrying about it. I didn't want to make an issue of it, but some of the other inmates scared me. They were so different from anyone I had ever known, even from a distance, and here we were, forced to live in each other's midst. Only a few of them seemed to have visitors—usually a wife and children who also seemed so different to me. In the beginning, the men occasionally muttered a few words to Jeb while we were with him—sometimes when we were standing in the kitchen having a cup of coffee—but they seldom spoke to me or the children. They hardly even looked at us. That made me feel very uncomfortable when they were around. For a long time it didn't occur to me that I might have had the same effect on them.

At Holabird, the inmates were allowed to wear their own clothes, so officially there were no uniforms. But it was hot in Baltimore in September and unofficially there was a sort of a uniform which both guards and inmates wore—with only a few distinctions. On the base the guards wore slacks and a shirt. The inmates wore slacks and sometimes a T-shirt, sometimes a shirt unbuttoned to the waist. Jeb was considered unusual because sometimes he wore an old knit sport shirt with his slacks.

The guards always were clean-shaven, but most of the inmates weren't. I don't know how they managed it, but a few of the inmates always had what looked like a three-day growth of beard—no more, no less.

Many of the men wore large, ornate expensive jewelry obviously made of solid gold. One man's pinky ring fascinated me although it was a long time before I got a good look at it. It was a huge gold ring in the shape of a Balinese dancer who had diamonds for eyes and a ruby in her navel. Some wore religious medallions on fine gold chains around their necks. The workmanship on all the jewelry was superb, but I just wasn't used to seeing so much gold on men.

Jeb never had been much of a cook at home, so he was at a disadvantage when it was his turn to take over the kitchen for the day. There was only one meal he ever made, and that was spaghetti. Well, he thought, that should be just fine. Jeb used a recipe he had learned from his mother, who used to make spaghetti a lot during the Depression. In those days most people couldn't afford meat, so Jeb's mother made her sauce with lots of onions, canned tomatoes, and some butter—nothing else. It bore no resemblance at all to the rich meat-and-bone-flavored sauce which the mothers of the other inmates probably had cooked in their childhood days.

As Jeb was cutting pounds and pounds of onions, he began to look forward to the meal. He was still a stranger to the other inmates, but he thought that once he began to fit into their routine, he might find it easier to talk to them.

Slowly, suspiciously, the other men came to the dining room. They sniffed the air and did not like what they smelled. When they approached the heaped-high plates, they clearly despised what they saw, and most of them turned and walked out. They didn't even want the green salad Jeb had tossed. A few men took a plate and sampled a forkful of spaghetti, but that was as far as they went. Most of them made terrible faces, then threw down their forks and left.

Jeb was crushed. All that cutting and chopping and mashing—for hours!—and now it all had to go in the garbage. Worse than that, he had lost his chance to find something in common with the men who were sharing his life.

But that poor, discredited spaghetti served a purpose after all. Instead of complimenting him on his cooking, the other men began to tease Jeb about it. That was all right because at least they were communicating. Finally one of the men offered to teach Jeb how to make one of the prisoners' favorite meals—roast lamb flavored with garlic and marinated vegetables—the next time he had to cook. It was a success! Jeb saved me a small portion, so I knew why.

The barrier was down—at least for Jeb. And even for me, to some extent. Now, when the children and I visited, a few of the inmates would join us in the kitchen for coffee. They still didn't speak to me directly, but they were very friendly with the children. They spoke to me through Jeb and they were very complimentary in their rough, teasing way.

"That's a nice family you've got there, Jeb," Angie, the leader, would say. "How did a dope like you ever get enough sense to marry a girl like your wife?"

Sometimes the teasing got rough, especially when two or three men joined in. They were amused by the reasons for Jeb's imprisonment. Watergate and everything related to it was tame in their eyes. It also was clumsy—they wouldn't have handled things that way. In their opinion, Jeb had done only one thing wrong: he got caught.

There was only one way to stop them when they were in a teasing mood. Jeb would smile and say, "Okay, now, that's enough. If you don't stop, the next time I cook, I'll make spaghetti."

11

I HAD BEEN THINKING a lot about fear because it had become so much a part of my life. I realize it probably is one of the most powerful forces in the world. Even though we aren't aware of it, we all fall into its grip. We just call it by other names.

I had seen many men—good men, decent men—stepping on other men to get ahead because they were afraid of failing. They called it "ambition" or "success." I had seen men who valued honor and integrity lower their standards to the point of outright deception because they were afraid of their superiors' disapproval. They called it "expediency" or "the name of the game." It occurred to me that the men I had distrusted—Haldeman, Dean, and Colson—were afraid of something, too, although I didn't know them well enough to understand what it was.

I had seen fear in the eyes of reporters and photographers who had no regard for our family's sensitivities. Not only had they stopped thinking of us as human beings; they didn't see themselves as human, either, not when they were on the job. They were too afraid of what would happen to them if they didn't "get the story."

The prosecutors were afraid of many things. The Watergate trial was the trial of the century, and they were afraid to lose it. They were out to get at the facts, no matter what the cost in terms of the persons involved. They called it "justice," but they forgot that justice exists for people, not the other way around.

Jill Vollner was afraid. She was young and she was the only woman in a high position on the prosecutors' staff. She *had* to do as well as the men! She *had* to win her superiors' approval! Only when she saw Jeb break down after his night in the county jail did she seem to moderate her own fears long enough to realize that he was a human being, just like her—that *he* was afraid and she was part of the reason for it. From that moment on, her attitude slowly began to change.

Still, she was extremely cautious. There I was, living in Washington only minutes away from the courthouse, yet at first she would not allow me to see Jeb when they broke for lunch. Finally she relented, but grudgingly, as if she was afraid I would somehow abandon our children and whisk Jeb off to Canada or Mexico.

In prison, I saw fear in the faces of both the guards and the prisoners. The inmates weren't in a position to disguise it, but the guards called it "law enforcement." Fear made it impossible for either one to look at the other with compassion.

Each marshal spent only two weeks at Holabird. Their rotation added a special uncertainty to life because the rules were enforced according to the disposition of the deputy in charge—the DIC—each week. Some were nice, some were cruel. When we had a good DIC, Jeb and I knew we and the children would be allowed to walk, in the company of a marshal, beyond the fenced-in section around the safe house. Usually a few other inmates would join us. Although the base was unoccupied, the grounds were kept beautifully, and it was such a relief to walk past the rose-bordered houses that once belonged to officers and their families. I used to pick some of the roses and bring them back to the dining room.

The kindness of some of the marshals helped to get us

through the bleak times. I remember one man, a Christian, who became a friend while taking a walk with us on a Sunday afternoon. Before we headed back for the safe house, he asked us to pray for his little boy who was soon to undergo surgery.

When we had a bad DIC, we knew that walks were out. Sometimes a vengeful DIC would suddenly order the guards to search every inmate's room. No one ever knew why, but the effect on the prisoners was devastating. Their spirits bobbed up and down according to the DIC of the week.

At Holabird, even my purse was searched every time I visited Jeb. I knew it was against the law, and once I even said to the guard, "You know that's illegal, don't you?"

He stopped going through my purse and looked at me coldly. "You have the choice of leaving or letting me search your purse," he said.

What else could I do? "All right," I said, and he went on with the search. He was afraid of me—not me, personally, because I think he knew me well enough to realize I wasn't dangerous. He was simply afraid of anything or anyone coming in from the outside.

Jeb used to get his exercise by jogging in the area outside the barracks. He ran with another prisoner, an Irish mafia hit man. One day they were almost finished with their laps when a large black car pulled up to the main gate at Holabird. The car had New York license plates. Immediately the guards from the safe house ran toward the two joggers, shouting, "Hurry up! Get inside—*fast!*" They were afraid the car might be carrying killers trying to fill the contract on Jeb's jogging companion. Fortunately, they were wrong. But that's how tense they were most of the time. Fear had completely distorted their personalities.

And what about me? I finally had to ask myself. *What was fear doing to me?*

It was arousing my mother instincts where Jeb was

concerned, and that wasn't good. I wanted to protect him—from the other prisoners, from the prosecutors, and from the defense attorneys who would try to discredit him as a trial witness. He seemed so totally defenseless that I wanted to step in and somehow do battle for him. Of course I couldn't. My covenant sisters were helping me understand my limitations, but it hurt. I was Jeb's wife, not his mother. I was human, not divine. And Jeb, even though a prisoner, was a man. I had to accept that. I had to stand back and allow him to handle his own situations.

My own fears were beginning to come out into the open, and I knew I would have to deal with them.

I? I did? No. Not I. That much was very clear. The reason I was frightened was that I was now aware of evil in the world. I saw it all around me. I don't know why I didn't see it earlier in my life because I know it was always there. But now that I could no longer hide from it or deny its presence, I was afraid of being overwhelmed by it.

I felt absolutely helpless. How could I prevent any of the other inmates from attacking my husband? How could I stop him from getting in the way of a guard's bullet? What could I do to soften the shock my children might feel upon seeing these men? What kind of conversations might they overhear? I could keep my children away from their father and perhaps even stay away myself because I couldn't stand the strain of my anxiety—but that would become an evil in itself. I had seen fear do such things to people.

No, of course I couldn't deal with evil. No human being could, although we had been trying ever since the time of Adam. I had enough understanding of the Bible to realize that we become evil by trying to oppose it. We aren't strong enough to win that battle, and that's why Jesus Christ came to win it for us.

Dear Lord! I prayed, *the battle has already been fought and won! Help me to realize that!*

The only thing I could do about my fears was to give them to God. He alone could deal with them. Jeb's safety and my children's sensitivities were in his hands, not mine.

It was an awkward moment for me because I had never done anything like that before. I enumerated my fears and gathered them together in my mind. Then I offered them to Christ. And I felt them being lifted—almost physically—from my hands. As I began to accept my own weakness I felt something give way in me. It was as if I had just taken a deep breath and let it all out in a long, wonderful sigh that shook my spirit loose from its tension.

A few days later, as Dr. Margaret Rockwell and her guide dog stepped off a curb, she was struck by a car turning the corner. It was twilight and the driver didn't see her. Dr. Rockwell was bruised and shaken, but she refused to follow her doctor's orders to remain in bed for more than a day. The second morning she got up at her usual time and left for her office escorted by her guide dog. She walked all the way just as she always did. At first I was angry at her for being so foolish, but then I realized that I had misinterpreted her behavior. She was neither foolish nor reckless. She was getting control of her fear because she knew that if she didn't it would control her. I couldn't help feeling that God was sending me a message through this wonderful woman. She refused to put another label on her fear. Instead she faced it, and in that way, she broke its power over her.

The next time I went to Holabird I caught myself stiffening when some of the inmates came in the kitchen. I was trying to hide my fear. *No, I thought, take a good look at it!*

These men were frightening, there was no use denying it. But they were more than that. They were lonely. They were rejected and treated with contempt by everyone who even knew they were alive. Society had no pity for their plight because it thought they deserved whatever they got. No one gave a serious thought to how they had become what they were. They had done terrible things, but terrible things must have been done to them to make such behavior possible. And, with it all, we shared the same humanity. We were brothers. God cared as much about them as he did about me—and perhaps even more, because their need for him was so much greater.

Suddenly they were no longer shadowy beings whose presence made me shiver. They were persons whose feelings were like mine. Their experiences were different, and I had allowed those experiences to separate us.

One day Jeb and I were in the dining room while some of the inmates were discussing the movie they had seen the night before. It was *The Godfather*, and they loved it. For some reason, it became the most natural thing in the world for me to speak to them.

"I read the book," I said, "but I was too scared to see the picture."

They laughed at that. Then one of them asked me what I thought of the book.

"Well, I thought it was probably exaggerated," I said.

No, it wasn't, they assured me. Gino, the man with the huge ring, told me that *The Godfather* was the way things were in his world. Exactly. "People get killed that easily," he said.

For the first time, we had spoken to each other without going through Jeb. As I got to know these men better, I realized that it simply wasn't their custom to speak directly to another man's wife—so they had been trying just as hard to get accustomed to me as I was to them. Anyway, the ice was broken. Gradually they began to talk to me more comfortably and without even realizing that they were doing something new and strange.

At first they teased me, just as they had done with Jeb. They delighted in shocking me with details about their way of life, and they knew exactly what my response would be.

For instance, when Sal, a small, elderly man, was carving a roast one day and I admired the way he did it, Gino poked the man standing next to him and said, loud enough for me to hear, "Isn't that beautiful? That's just the way he sliced up Little Joey." I gasped and they laughed like children.

But underneath the teasing was something else—a hunger to share in our family. Most of these men had no family other than their criminal organization. They spoke of women, and sometimes of wives and children, but usually as persons they had known somewhere in their distant pasts. Very few wives and children showed up during visiting hours. In some of the rooms, there were photographs of women, and sometimes women with children, but I seldom learned who they were.

One of the men became especially close to Jeb. He was an enormous man, well over 6 feet tall and about 220 pounds of solid muscle which he kept developing in the weight-lifting room. His name was Skitch. He was in his midthirties and had spent 12 years of his adult life in jail. He was married and had a little boy about Stuart's age who was twice Stuart's size.

We used to see Skitch's wife and son a lot when we first began visiting Jeb at Holabird. They kept to themselves and spent most of their time in Skitch's room. But our children became acquainted, and then we did.

Skitch's son, whose name was Bruce, was a violent child who needed a great deal of attention. He obviously had suffered severe personality distortions from the long absences of his father. He and his mother also had moved around a lot because it wasn't safe for them to remain very long in one place. Bruce wasn't accustomed to playing with other children. We used to bring two bikes for the children to ride, and Bruce was not content to ask whether he could ride one, too. Instead, he simply walked up to the bike and tried to wrench it from the rider's hands. He was too much for Stuart, but Whitney and Justin were wonderfully patient with him.

They would pry his fingers off the bike and tell him he was welcome to ride it if he would wait his turn. When Bruce got the bike, however, he never wanted to give it up.

One day Bruce tackled me as I was walking on the grass outside in the fenced yard. If one of my own children had done it, he would have let me go the moment he made his point—but not Bruce. He held on so tight I knew I was going to fall. I had to reach down and try to pry him loose while I tried to reason with him. My anger left me the moment I looked into his eyes and saw how happy he was because I was talking to him. He wanted attention and didn't know any other way to get it.

Bruce had absolutely no control over his temper, and we had to watch him when he was with Stuart. Once he got so angry that he picked up a piece of rope and tried to strangle Stuart with it. Physical violence was as natural to him as angry words are to most other children.

Jean, Skitch's wife, was a beautiful woman. Her clothes were colorful and extreme, but she had the figure for them. Until Bruce began to play with our children, she seemed to want nothing to do with us, but, then, I think she began to regard us almost as babysitters who gave her a chance to be alone with her husband. Gradually she began to talk to me, although it was difficult for both of us to have any kind of conversation. Jean was very guarded about her life because she lived in constant danger, even though the government had arranged a new identity for her and her son. Jeb told me that a few weeks earlier machinegun bullets had smashed through the windshield of her car while she and Bruce were in it. They were not hurt, but their fear intensified. So there wasn't much she could tell me about herself and I couldn't very well ask questions. Our motherhood seemed to be the only common ground on which we could stand with any degree of comfort—that and the fact that both of us wanted our husbands home again.

In their way, Skitch and Jean were concerned about their

son, but there wasn't much they could do to help him. They were too worn out by their own problems to give him the patient care and love he so evidently needed.

Money was about the only problem they didn't have. From what we could see, Jean and Bruce were well dressed, well fed and had everything they needed. They rented an apartment in the Baltimore area to be near Skitch. We didn't know the details of Skitch's arrangement with the government, but apparently some kind of monthly allowance was part of it.

When you first hear about such things as "a new identity," you think of it as a good and generous idea. But in practice it isn't—because it doesn't work. The men at Holabird would be given new, falsified birth certificates and other means of identification before they were released. When they were released they would be sent to a part of the country where they were not likely to be known. But from there on, it was up to them.

It should have been so simple. All these men had to do was fade into their new identities and live a quiet, peaceful life. The trouble is, nobody taught them how to behave differently. They have the same habits, the same inclinations, the same backgrounds. The only kind of work they know is crime. They try to get a job but they run into difficulties: no one wants to hire them because they don't really have any useful skills. And so, gradually, they drift back into the old meeting places, and finally someone recognizes them. Before long, they are dead.

These men didn't try to fool themselves. They had no real hopes for a new identity, but they were going along with the idea for as long as it would last. "They'll get us," Gino told me. "We all walk with one eye looking behind us —but they'll get us. You won't know it. You'll read something in the paper about some guy who got knocked off for no good reason and the police won't be able to find out who did it. That'll be one of us."

I shivered, but this time, it was because I cared about what happened to Gino.

Gino cared about us, too. One day while I was with Jeb in his room, we heard the sound of heavy-booted feet pounding down the hall in our direction. My throat went dry, and as the door was flung open by the DIC, I felt my stomach turn over.

"What's she doing here?" the DIC shouted, pointing to me.

"This is my wife," Jeb explained calmly. "She's visiting."

"Get her out of here!" he ordered. "No women allowed in your room!"

Jeb and I looked at each other in confusion. No one had ever told us that. In fact, it was a DIC who first explained the visiting rules to me and told me I could sit with Jeb in his room. Jeb tried to explain that to the DIC, who stubbornly refused to listen. He kept yelling at me to get out.

It was a difficult situation for us because we could demand our "rights" only up to a point, and the point varied with the disposition of the DIC.

Finally, Jeb suggested that he and the DIC consult the visiting regulations which were printed in a notebook in the warden's office. He said we would abide by them, whatever they were, and the DIC agreed.

They were just leaving the room when tiny Gino rushed up to the DIC and shook his fist in his face. "You leave my friends alone," he screamed. "Don't you bother them! You leave my friends alone!"

"It's all right, Gino," Jeb assured him, trying to calm him down. The DIC was frightened by the fury of Gino's attack.

Two more guards rushed up behind Gino and the moment they put their hands on him, he went wild. "You leave my friends alone," he kept shouting, faster and faster. In his rage, he was more than the two guards and the DIC could handle and they called for help. We could hear more guards running down the hall.

Suddenly Gino's body became rigid and he began to foam at the mouth. "He's sick!" I cried out, realizing he was having some kind of attack. More guards seized him and pulled him away from the room and down the hall. We were not allowed to go with him, but we could hear the sounds of struggle as the guards tried to subdue him, and all the while, Gino kept repeating, "These are my friends! These are my friends!"

I felt tears on my face, and I was sick with anger. Jeb put his arm around me until I gained control of myself. We tried to explain to ourselves what had happened, but it was very difficult. How do you explain the things people do through fear?

When the rule book was consulted, it confirmed my "right" to be in Jeb's room. But—perhaps just to save face— the DIC decreed that the door must always be left open while we were there. A little bit of newfound privacy was taken away.

We did not see Gino for several weeks. He was hospitalized and later underwent brain surgery for an ailment that is similar to epilepsy. While he was recovering, he developed some stomach problems and had two abdominal operations.

A lot of the inmates at Holabird, like those at Allenwood, were trying to sleep their way through their misery. Heavy tranquilizers—such as the Thorazine I've mentioned —were readily available. I never got to know some of the men because they spent all their time in bed in their rooms, and many who were up and around were in a stupor. Once I watched in horror as Skitch came into the kitchen without recognizing us, picked up a mug in one hand and the coffee pot in the other, and tried to pour himself a cup of coffee. He missed the cup by about 4 inches and the hot liquid splashed onto the floor. Skitch never even noticed it. He put the pot down and shuffled into the dining room where he sat in a chair holding his empty mug as if it were full.

When we first knew him, Skitch used every kind of drugs he could get his hands on. That was his way of dealing with his anger and frustration. He was a very discouraged, pessimistic man who would not allow himself to hope for anything good. If Jeb said, "Hey, what a nice day, Skitch," he would answer, "Yeah—but it'll rain."

Skitch was the man who jogged with Jeb. He began doing it because he was interested in keeping his big body in good condition, but, as the two men ran around and around the small area in front of the safe house, they would talk to break up the monotony of their exercise. Little by little, Skitch opened up to Jeb. He told him about his concern for his wife and child. He had many more years to serve before he would become eligible for parole, and he had no idea where he would be sent to prison after Holabird was phased out. He hoped he wouldn't be sent too far away, where Jean and Bruce would find it hard to visit him. He was confused by the angry feelings inside himself. If he couldn't smash a wall with his fist or hit somebody, he was at a loss.

"What do you do when you get mad, Jeb?" he would ask.

And for the first time in his life, Jeb began to witness. He told Skitch that he prayed to the Lord to take the anger from him and give him peace. He didn't know how Skitch would react to that. For the rest of the laps, the two men ran side by side, saying nothing.

Skitch continued to run with Jeb every day, and now he began to ask more questions—about prayer, about God, about Jesus. He really was interested.

Skitch and his family were becoming very important to all of us. On the way home from Holabird, the children and I used to try to figure out different ways of dealing with the obstreperous Bruce. We wanted to show him we loved him, but without letting him bully us. At dinner every night, the children included him in their prayers. Jeb was trying to educate Skitch in the ways of the parole board so that when it was time for him to make out his application he would know what he was doing.

Little by little, change began to occur. Bruce never would be a quiet child, but some of his hostility was abating. His mother had bought him a bike of his own, which he even allowed our children to ride. That was a big step for him to take! He didn't lose his temper as often, nor did he go into a rage when he wasn't the center of attention. He seemed to love being with our older boys.

I noticed that Skitch was more alert than he used to be, and Jeb confirmed my hope that he wasn't using as many tranquilizers. At least, he was willing to try another way of handling his anger. We weren't sure, but we thought perhaps he was praying—in his own fashion.

On Hallowe'en, I brought Jeb some candy and fruit wrapped up in orange and black napkins—and as an afterthought I also brought a plastic pumpkin filled with candy for the other inmates. I put it on the dining room table, expecting everyone to help himself—which was a foolish thing to do. I had forgotten that I wasn't at home, offering goodies to friends and children who were accustomed to such things. A few minutes later, when I passed the dining room, I noticed that the pumpkin was gone. The men couldn't have helped themselves in that short amount of time. Someone had taken the whole pumpkin for himself.

Jeb knew who it was. He went upstairs and came back in a few minutes with the pumpkin. Eddie, a small, sixtyish, grumpy man who rarely left his room, had taken it. He didn't understand what it meant to share, probably because no one had ever given him anything, so when he saw something he wanted, he took it before someone else did. When Jeb retrieved the pumpkin from him, he told him to come downstairs and take some of the candy for himself, but he never showed up.

Holidays in prison were devastating. The few families who were able to get together were saddened by their memories of happier times, and those who had no visitors avoided the company of those who did.

I didn't know what to plan for Thanksgiving Day. We would be able to spend it with Jeb, and for that I was grateful, but the rules had been changed again and visitors were no longer allowed to eat with the inmates. We could bring sandwiches and soda for ourselves, but nothing more. Fortunately, the restrictions were suspended for the holiday, and we were told that the inmates would prepare a turkey dinner for everyone.

It was not a very happy occasion, but that wasn't the fault of anyone present. Patti Colson brought linen tablecloths and napkins for the dining room tables and put a small bouquet of flowers on each one. My covenant sisters sent packages of home-baked cookies and a short holiday message to each inmate. Patti and Chuck Colson ate in the dining room with most of the other inmates, but there were too many in our family to squeeze in, so we ate upstairs on the Ping-Pong table in the recreation room.

The turkey, stuffed with a spicy dressing, was delicious. Later, when we returned to Jeb's room, Skitch came by and gave us a pumpkin pie he had made for us.

Some of the inmates didn't come down to dinner, so after everyone had eaten the children and I went to their rooms to deliver our packages of cookies. Some of the men didn't answer us when we called to them—whether they were asleep or just pretending, we couldn't tell—so we left the packages at the door. One man I had never seen before because he was always asleep in his room, got up out of bed and stumbled to the door. He had a three-day beard and his clothes were crumpled. He seemed not to comprehend when we wished him a happy Thanksgiving and asked God to bless him, but he took the package we held out to him and nodded drowsily.

An hour later, we saw the same man down in the dining

room and we almost didn't recognize him. He had washed and shaved and put on fresh clothes. His eyes were bright and alert, and he was eating a cookie from the package he held tightly in his hand. When I saw that such a small gift had given him so much pleasure, I wished I could give him something—anything—more.

Was it possible, I wondered, that we found ourselves at Holabird for reasons beyond those of its convenience to our home? Was God finding some use for us even in the midst of our own anxiety?

It seemed to me that, if he was, he didn't expect us to be more than what we were—a Christian family. That surprised me. Somehow I always thought God would make use of me in a different way. I assumed he would tap me on the shoulder one day and want me to make a speech describing how I felt about him—and I shrank from the prospect. Perhaps I was too new a Christian, but I just wasn't comfortable putting my love for my Lord into words. It never occurred to me that there were other ways to speak, ways that were fully acceptable to God and completely intelligible to other people.

There was something I wanted to tell these men. I wanted them to know that I loved them. But more than that, I wanted them to know God was loving them through me, through Jeb and through our children. He hadn't given up on them. He knew what they were suffering and wanted to comfort them. He asked nothing but the chance to minister to their hurts.

That was the only gift I could give my brothers. But I knew its value because the same gift had already been given to me—by my husband and children, by our friends, and by the letters which still came to our home offering prayers for strength and words of love.

Oh, Lord, I prayed, *let me pass on your gift!*

12

AMONG THE INMATES, there were divisions and rivalries. The men from other countries did not get along with the Mafia men—and even within the Mafia, there were factions. Some were Irish Mafia and some were Italian Mafia. I had read about Mafia activities in books and newspapers but I had never taken them seriously. I thought they were figments of a good writer's imagination. But the Holabird inmates assured me that most of what I had read was true.

When Jeb entered Holabird, the leader of the Mafia men was a man called Angelo. He was soft spoken and small in stature, but something about his manner was threatening and he frightened me more than the others.

Angelo had almost finished his sentence and his parole was supposed to begin sometime in October. Toward the end of September, he began making plans for his release. In the company of two marshals, he went to downtown Baltimore to a Thunderbird dealer and bought a beautiful new car so he could leave Holabird in style. He was quite upset when the marshals told him he would not be allowed to bring the car back to Holabird with him. It would have to wait at the dealer's until he was released.

Angelo was sulking when I saw him that afternoon.

"I hear you bought a new car, Angelo," I said. "You must be very excited about it."

"Yeah," he grumbled moodily.

"What does it look like?"

"Freedom," he said.

"Aren't you worried about all those car payments?" I said. "I mean, that's a big load to be carrying when you get out."

"Nah, that's no problem—I paid cash," he said.

Money was never a problem to most of these men. Even though they dressed in T-shirts and rumpled slacks, it wasn't because they didn't have clothes. In the closets of their rooms I saw outfit after outfit, all of them handsomely tailored. On the closet floors were several pairs of Gucci shoes, hardly worn.

Naturally Angelo expected to be released on October 1. I couldn't blame him. He wanted to get out of there as much as anybody. But the day passed without any word from the head marshal, a man the inmates nicknamed "Colonel Klink" after the character on "Hogan's Heroes" TV show. Then another day and another day passed, and still no word. The next time I came to visit, I met Angelo in the hall outside the marshal's office and he was furious.

"What's the matter?" I said.

His face and neck were getting redder as I watched him. "They can't let me out when they said they would," he said, clenching his teeth. "Something about the paperwork—they didn't get it done yet."

I couldn't believe it, yet it was true. Angelo's release papers were caught up in bureaucratic red tape and no one was making any effort to untangle them. Meanwhile he remained a prisoner, even though he had served his sentence.

"Oh, Angelo," I said, "don't you see? They're trying to make you lose your cool. Please, don't let them do this to you! Try to hold on."

He nodded and reached out to pat my shoulder reassuringly. Then, without another word, he walked away.

E

The next week I saw a huge hole in the plaster wall just inside the front door of the building. "What happened?" I asked the guard at the door.

He shrugged. "Angelo. He got mad and put his fist through the wall."

"His release papers still didn't come through?" I said.

"Not yet," he said, with as much concern as if he were telling me that the morning newspaper hadn't arrived that day.

Angelo's papers didn't come through for another four weeks. He served a total of six extra weeks as a prisoner.

Not long after Angelo left, another prisoner was brought to Holabird, and immediately the OC inmates accepted him as their new leader. His name was Leo. He was a tall, heavy-set man and very nervous. His hands were never still and his eyes constantly darted around the room. Perhaps it was this constant agitation that made him seem even more threatening than Angelo. Angelo, however, never had any visitors and spent much of his time in his room. Leo had a wife who came to see him frequently. She was a very attractive woman in her midforties.

When the Watergate trial began early in October, Jeb had to spend more of his time at the prosecutors' offices. Finally Jill Vollner, the prosecutor working with Jeb, seemed to believe him. Now they had to prepare him for the witness stand where he would be led through his testimony by Jill Vollner and then cross-examined by defense attorneys for John Mitchell, Bob Haldeman, John Erlichman, Kenneth Parkinson, and Robert Mardian. These attorneys were skillful men who would try their best to discredit Jeb and John Dean, the prosecution's key witnesses, so it was important for them to know their facts and the sequence of events better than they knew their own names. Over and over Jill Vollner took Jeb through the whole Watergate story, which was like rubbing salt in his wounds. But there was no other way. When he could tell his story backward as well as forward, a team of prosecutors took the part of the defense attorneys firing question after question at him. They covered every possibility.

Jill Vollner had relented and was allowing me to spend some lunch hours with Jeb. I used to bring a picnic basket to the courthouse and we would eat in a room where they stored extra desks and chairs. Sometimes, when we had a considerate marshal, we took our picnic basket out on the Smithsonian Mall in front of the National Gallery of Art. We would spread a blanket on the grass and enjoy the warm autumn sun and the lovely fall colors of the leaves against the blue sky. Usually the marshal stayed a little apart, giving us a few special moments of peace together. It didn't seem possible that a short time later we would be back in the courtroom, tense and anxious.

October 17 was our fifteenth wedding anniversary. Five years earlier, on our tenth anniversary, I was at home with the children in California and Jeb was in the White House mess hall, so at least now we were not quite that far apart. I wanted to do something special to mark the occasion.

I was fortunate that the press was so busy chasing after some of the more recognizable persons involved in the trial that usually I was able to go in and out of the courthouse without any trouble. My only difficulty was protecting myself from the jostling that was unavoidable as I tried to push my way through the thick wall of people with cameras, lights, and microphones. I solved that problem by carrying a large, square pocketbook made of wood and decorated with hand-painted birds. It served as a shield and, if necessary, a weapon.

On October 17, I came to the courthouse at my usual time—a little before 10 A.M.—with my usual picnic basket and pocketbook. When the court broke for lunch, at noon, I met Jeb and a marshal in the furniture storage room and began unpacking our lunch. I brought along a few special celebratory items—a linen tablecloth, linen napkins, and a candle—and I set our "table" on one of the old desks. The marshal usually left us alone for about twenty minutes, so I waited until he was gone and then I served lunch. We had peanut butter and jelly sandwiches—and champagne. I brought the champagne in a large vacuum bottle which everyone assumed contained coffee.

So much about the Watergate trial seemed unreal to me. I had not seen the five defendants in a very long time, and I had known them under entirely different circumstances. There were many changes, but I couldn't be sure who had changed the most, we or they. Bob Haldeman came up to me in the corridor outside the courtroom and was friendlier than he had ever been to me. He went right back into the court-room to get his wife, Jo, who was talking to someone else, and brought her to see me. Jo, as always, was concerned and thoughtful.

I saw John Mitchell, too. One day, when he saw that no one was watching him, he took my arm and we walked around a corner where we could have a few words without being overheard. He wanted to know how the children were getting along. I still loved this man, and I could understand Jeb's discomfort in the knowledge that his testimony was going to hurt Mitchell.

Kenneth Parkinson made the best appearance of all the defendants. Every day he came to court dressed in a con-servative business suit, his hair neatly trimmed and combed, and his shoes shined. He listened attentively to everything that was said and never glowered or frowned at any of the testimony. Robert Mardian was exactly the opposite. His be-havior was crude and abusive. Passing Jeb in the corridor just before Jeb was to take the stand for the first time, he said, "You lousy son of a bitch!" in a loud, hoarse whisper.

Jeb was on the stand for five days. He never faltered or broke once, no matter how hard the defense attorneys ham-mered at him. Jill Vollner had done her job well.

In many ways, I felt that we were more fortunate than most of the others involved in the trial. We had so much help and such wonderful support at a time when we desperately needed it. Each day Jeb was on the stand, one of my covenant sisters sat next to me in the courtroom. When the court broke for lunch, I always saw more dear familiar faces in the audience, and in the corridor I was held by loving arms. Some of our friends joined us in the storage room for lunch and brought homemade breads and fruit and cookies for us to eat. I felt Jesus Christ in every smile, every touch, every reassuring word, and I will never forget the comfort I found in his presence right in the midst of all those people.

I also had had a small personal victory. I had let go of my husband so that he could fight his own battle. The yearning to protect him was gone, replaced by the sure faith that God would take care of him far better than anyone else ever could. I was proud of Jeb on the witness stand. And I was very relieved when the five days were over. That was a part of Watergate we could now put behind us.

Most people probably never will find themselves in a courtroom, and if it hadn't been for Watergate I probably never would have been in one either. Yet my father is a lawyer, and I had always been interested in law. When I was a student at Berkeley I took courses in law and found them fascinating. My professors encouraged me to go on to other law courses, and there were times when I thought I might study to become a lawyer.

Like many other women, now and then when I was changing diapers or trying to get the children interested in some indoor diversions on a rainy day, I would sigh over my lost opportunities and imagine myself pleading my client's case before a judge. Occasionally I thought about going back to school when the children were older.

Part of me had a great curiosity about the legal proceedings I was to watch each day I attended the Watergate trial. This was no theoretical interpretation of justice. This was real. It was The Law in practice, not law in a textbook. And what a difference there is between the two.

I had loved the study of law. I was disillusioned by The Law. In my college textbooks, justice was the result of an evaluation of the positions of different people, all of whom were equal. If two men committed similar crimes, they paid similar penalties to society. Not so with The Law. It was prejudiced, partial, and easily impressed. That was very evident in the outcome of the Watergate trial.

Bob Haldeman, John Mitchell, John Erlichman, and Robert Mardian were found guilty. Kenneth Parkinson was acquitted. I could not help but feel that the courtroom demeanor of the defendants had a lot to do with the verdicts. I knew, from Jeb, that Kenneth Parkinson had known about the cover-up. He had given Jeb legal counsel when Jeb first thought about going to the prosecutors. In fact, this was the reason Jeb waited so long to hire his own lawyers. But Kenneth Parkinson was a model of good behavior throughout the trial. Robert Mardian was not, and a jury could not have helped noticing the difference. When the verdict was announced, Robert Mardian's wife even made an obscene gesture to the judge.

I had seen, too, how well a trial is rehearsed. I knew all the reasons for it, and yet I found the process disappointing. I used to think that testimony was a matter of telling the truth as a person saw or experienced it. Now I realized that it had been refined into a performance. Somehow it seemed that justice got lost in all these maneuvers. Where was the unvarying measure against which a person was held to determine his guilt or innocence? From where I sat, it seemed that the measure was too easily telescoped to fit the persons involved.

We thought Jeb would be sent back to Allenwood after he gave his testimony, but the prosecutors wanted to keep him close to Washington in case he was recalled to the stand.

On November 5, the day after Jeb finished testifying, he was forty years old. He didn't know it, but the inmates at Holabird followed a certain routine for celebrating birthdays. In the morning Jeb was told to go out and buy a birthday cake. He was surprised because he thought it would be more appropriate for the other men to buy a cake for the one who had the birthday, but that wasn't the way they did things. So out Jeb went, escorted by two federal marshals. They went to a bakery and waited there while a sheet cake was decorated with icing that spelled out "HAPPY BIRTHDAY TO JEB." He was so angry he didn't eat a piece of it, but the other men enjoyed it thoroughly.

I was grateful for the flexibility of our children. They were great favorites with the other inmates and accepted them easily. Paulo, a former follower of Fidel Castro, was in on a drug-smuggling charge, and his attentions to the children sometimes made me uneasy. I didn't like the way he always tried to get them to come to his room, but they had the good sense never to go in alone. Then I learned that Paulo was helping Whit with his Spanish. I felt ashamed of my suspicions and prayed to be forgiven.

We had something to learn from our children. We were so concerned with being able to give to these prisoners that we had forgotten how important it was to receive from them. They too had gifts for us—gifts from an entirely different culture, but nevertheless sincerely offered. One day, Whitney came into the kitchen while I was making coffee and said, "Hey, Mom, do you know what Paulo just taught me?"

"What?" I asked.

"He showed me what to do if a guy came up behind me and grabbed me around the neck—a guy who's bigger than I am."

What a horrible idea! I thought. Then I caught myself. From my point of view it *was* horrible, but not from Paulo's. It was the sort of thing that was very likely to happen in

Paulo's life, so why shouldn't he think it might happen to Whit, too? He liked Whit, and the only thing he could give him as a token of his friendship was a lesson in self-defense.

"Here, let me show you how it works," Whit said, coming around in front of me. "You come up and grab me around the neck from behind." I did the best I could, but I'm afraid I wasn't much of a menace. Nevertheless I could understand what Whitney was doing, and it worked. He was very pleased.

Gino came back near the end of November. He was pale and weak from so much surgery, and I noticed that his wife never came to see him anymore. He used to visit us in Jeb's room and one day he began talking about his wife. He said she was thinking of divorcing him.

"Isn't there anything you can do to change her mind?" I said.

"I don't think so," he said. "She's mad at me because I've got other women."

I didn't know quite what to say.

"She doesn't like it because I buy houses for some of them," he said.

"Gino, I don't blame her," I said. I wasn't sure how far I could go with these men. They had come a long way by talking to me as they did, but I wasn't sure they were ready to hear me disagree with them. I chose my words as carefully as I could. "That's the hardest thing for a woman to take from a man she loves," I said. "It makes her feel so worthless."

He listened, so I went on. I told him how I would have felt if my husband had done something like that to me, and he seemed to understand. He asked me if I thought his wife would change her mind about divorcing him if he promised to give up his other women. I said I thought she might—and at least it was worth trying. I felt that anything was worth trying if it would save a marriage.

It looked as if Jeb would still be at Holabird for Christmas, which was very good for us. We were especially touched when Leo invited our family and the Colsons to have Christmas dinner with his group of inmates—the OC.

For several days before Christmas, the men were busy making preparations. They went out often to shop for food and Christmas decorations and there was an atmosphere of excitement throughout the safe house.

On Christmas morning, the children and I had breakfast with the Gillespies and then left for Holabird. We arrived there a little after 1 P.M. As we went through the gates I remembered a Christmas season two years ago when we were invited to a Christmas breakfast at the White House. Then, too, we went past armed guards at every door. It seemed that wherever you went in the system you found fear.

There were too many of us to fit in the dining room, so we ate upstairs in the recreation room. Dinner was served on the Ping-Pong table. Only the Mafia group and their guests were present. The international group ate downstairs in the dining room. John Dean ate in his room. Herb Kalmbach ate with the international group.

I suppose we expected too much. We had caught some of the prisoners' excitement and had visions of a leisurely, friendly gathering in a lovely sitting. But the recreation room was still the same dirty room with bare windows and a scuffed floor. On other days I wouldn't have minded it, but somehow on Christmas, it made me feel as if I were going to choke. The inmates had done the best they could with what they had. They covered the table with white sheets and hung sheets at the windows where curtains should have been. They decorated the table with plastic Christmas ornaments and draped tinsel from everything that would hold it, but still the room was sterile and forelorn.

There were seventeen of us—six from our family; Chuck and Patti Colson and Chuck's mother; Gino, his wife, and little girl; Leo and his wife; Dave—who had stayed up all night cooking—his girlfriend, and her child. Skitch should have been there, but he stayed in his room most of the day. His wife was away, spending the holidays with relatives, and I think the company of other families made him feel too lonely.

Jeb and I thought we might find the right moment to say grace before dinner, which would have been particularly appropriate. We were so grateful to be able to spend this day together and we just assumed that the others felt the same way. But the moment the food appeared, most of the other inmates helped themselves and began eating, without waiting for anyone else. So Jeb and the children and I muttered a few words of thanksgiving at our end of the table.

The meal itself was exquisitely prepared and served. Our first course was an antipasto, the finest and most elaborate I have ever seen or eaten. Each slice of meat and cheese was rolled or folded, and each piece of vegetable was artistically arranged. The colors of the olives, ham, fish, salami, artichokes, carrots, parsley, melons, tomatoes, and peppers were irresistible.

Next came huge pans of lasagne and a salad. Everyone ate so much of it that no one could take more than a bite of the turkey that had been added to the meal as a gesture to the Colsons and us. For desert we had a rich lemon cake.

In the world I had known, guests would have lingered over such a meal, enjoying the opportunity to relax and talk to each other. But I was not in that world now. Most of the people in that room did not know what it meant to relax. The men held their plates up close to their chins and shoveled the food into their mouths, their eyes keeping guard on the right and the left. Leo didn't even sit down. He ate standing up, bolting his food as quickly as he could, as if the act of eating was a vulnerability he could not afford. "He always eats like this," his wife Dorothy said, apologetically. "Isn't it terrible!" It *was* terrible—because it reminded me that this man lived under the threat of death every moment.

I noticed that Gino was going out of his way to be pleasant to his wife. But, she, unaccustomed to the attention, kept rejecting him. Every now and then their voices would rise in anger. The other men didn't talk to the women at all. Puzzled by their behavior, our children were quieter than usual. Jeb and I made a few attempts at conversation, but felt too awkward to continue.

Chuck Colson was hard to understand. He seemed to take on the characteristics of the people around him. He was under attack for his claim that he had had a conversion, but I believed him. When he was with Christians, he seemed to be a Christian. Yet I learned from Jeb that there were times when he slipped back into the same bad habits that he had exhibited in the White House. I suppose I was like a lot of other people who were impatient with him because he didn't seem to change after becoming a Christian. I had to remind myself that I was a pretty new Christian too.

Change takes a long time—as I well knew—and some of us have to do a lot of growing on the inside before it becomes visible on the outside. The little signs become visible first, and if we aren't sensitive to them we may miss them entirely. In Chuck Colson, there were many little signs. He was serious about reading his Bible and as many Christian books as he could get his hands on. He was searching himself and at the same time opening himself up to God. That took courage—and faith.

When everyone had had enough to eat, the dinner was over. We went back to Jeb's room and spent the rest of the day there. It was so different from the happy, laughing, embracing Christmases we had known. We were too sad to try to cheer each other. This was to have been a special Christmas for us because we had found Christ, yet suddenly he seemed far away. Had he been unable to get past the guards at Holabird that day?

On the way home, I felt a growing sense of alarm. I was

cut off from God! I didn't know how to get back in touch with him.

The children and I had a small Christmas tree at home. At first I wasn't going to have one at all because I couldn't stand the thought of decorating it without Jeb. But then I realized that the children needed a tree this year more than ever. Christmas night, after the children went to bed, I sat in the living room with the tree lights on, feeling very lost and lonely. Even here in our home, I couldn't find God.

What on earth was I going to do without him? The old fears began to return. I rediscovered all my former suspicions and anxieties about Holabird. How long would Jeb be safe there? For some ridiculous reason I had had the feeling that Jeb would be home sometime in January. I couldn't account for it because by January he would have been in prison seven months—not even the ten months we once had hoped would be enough. Now I had to get the idea out of my mind.

I didn't know when Jeb would be coming home, but it would not be soon. I had to begin facing the fact that loneliness and I were going to be together for a long time to come.

13

BEING ALIENATED FROM GOD was the most desolate feeling I have ever known. It was worse than never having known his nearness because now I knew how helpless I was without him.

I realize that other people go through this from time to time, and I have no idea where or how they find God again. I only know that for me nothing seemed to work. I still had the love and support of my covenant sisters, but it was not the same. Each Sunday, when I attended church before going to Holabird, I found acceptance and comfort, but something was missing. It was the custom of one of the ushers, Carl Easten, to give me his white carnation after the service so I would have a flower to wear when I visited Jeb, and as I pinned it on my coat that Sunday after Christmas, I had all I could do to keep from crying because I yearned so desperately for the One in whose name the flower was given. I tried spending more time alone reading my Bible, but the guidance was gone and no new insights came from the words. I prayed—not with confidence, but with dread that the answer might not come.

When the answer came, it was startling in its simplicity. *I could not find God—he would find me.* And then I understood that this was the way it always had been.

He found me gently, quietly, with no fanfare. I was getting ready for bed one night and wondering what was going to happen to Jeb. The Watergate trial had ended for him on New Year's Day when the verdicts were handed down. He found it hard to live with the uncertainty of not knowing how long he would be kept at Holabird, and he told me he was thinking of requesting his transfer back to Allenwood. I didn't think that was a very good idea because somehow I felt Holabird was a better place for him to be.

How strange, I thought, *that I should find anything good about a prison.*

A message was coming into my mind. The words were forming so distinctly that I sat down at my desk and began writing them out: *I am beginning to think Jeb may need to stay at Holabird awhile. In November and December I prayed for a mid-January release, but now I see his ministry to the others. They are opening up. And Jeb needs the forced quiet to think and grow and get a firm hold on himself as an independent Christian man before he returns to the world. Thank you, God, for Holabird!*

The words were not mine, but God's, and I knew they had come to me through the Holy Spirit.

The pieces began to fall into place. I had wanted Jeb's release so badly that I was blind to what was happening to him in prison. He needed the time, the quiet—even the boredom—in which to get his thoughts together. At Holabird, he had a room to himself and so far, at least, there still was a door to it. He could study, he could read, he could get some perspective on his life. At Allenwood, where he slept in a dormitory with forty-nine other men, there were too many noises and other distractions for him to think. The large number of inmates at Allenwood also made close relationships impossible. Holabird, with eighteen prisoners, gave Jeb an opportunity to know these men and understand what they were going through. He could see Herb Kalmbach suffering in his shame, and Skitch being consumed by his rage. He was constantly reminded that it was God who had sustained him, and nothing he or we had done.

There were other reasons why I could thank God for Holabird. We could actually see God reaching out to the inmates. Skitch was not off drugs entirely, but he used them far less frequently. Now, if Jeb said, "Hey, it's a nice day!" Skitch agreed. He was even thinking about his future instead of resigning himself to the probability that he didn't have one. When he and Jeb were outside running, he began to ask Jeb what he thought he could do after he got out to avoid becoming involved in a life of crime again.

Eddie, the man who taught Jeb how to cook, used to have no expectations at all. On Christmas day, when the children and I went from door to door with a Christmas note for each man, we found a drawing of a hanging man on Eddie's door. We knocked and gave him the note, anyway. I mentioned the drawing and said it was awful. Later that day, the drawing was gone, and the next time we came to visit, Eddie greeted us with a smile. Gino and his wife, clumsy though they were, were trying to rebuild their marriage.

The most important change was that all the other inmates were accepting us into their midst, even though we didn't always understand each other. We were becoming a family. We were learning to accept each other's differences and to love each other exactly as we were. We were concerned with what happened to each other.

Yes, I realized, God had been present at Holabird on Christmas Day. I don't know how many other people were aware of that. I certainly wasn't. I had made the mistake of looking at the surroundings—which were undeniably grim—instead of in the hearts of those who sat around our Ping-Pong table. The very fact that all of us were together was the most exciting, dramatic proof of God's presence among us. I had been present at a miracle and didn't even know it!

"Oh, Jesus!" I prayed, "I'm so glad you found me again!" That night I slept more peacefully than I had in a long time.

Holabird was unmistakably closing down. The visiting

hours were shortened. More disturbing was the rumor that the doors were going to be taken off the rooms.

Probably Jeb would have been sent back to Allenwood as soon as the trial ended if it hadn't been for John Dean and whatever arrangement he had made with the prosecutors. As long as he wasn't in a prison, the other prosecution witnesses couldn't very well be sent to one. So they all shared in Dean's benefits.

On the morning of January 7 the phone woke me up early. I was still groggy when I heard a voice I remembered from Allenwood. It was Jim Benjamin, a man who had a bunk near Jeb's. He told me he had been released early because some of the other inmates were planning to "get him." The prison officials put him in a solitary confinement cell in Lewisburg for a few days and then decided to let him out because he was due for parole soon anyway. He called to warn me that the same inmates had threatened to kill Jeb if he came back to Allenwood.

I sat there holding the phone, trying to shake my head free of its numbness. I knew better than to ask "Why?" Before I had ever been inside a prison I would have said, "Why would anyone want to kill Jeb?" but having known some of the men at Allenwood and having heard from Jeb about the nighttime attacks on sleeping inmates I realized that the answer would have been "Why *not?*" Prison is not a place for rationality. Why not kill or beat up someone like Jim Benjamin, a man so troubled by the disintegration of his family that he could not deal with the other prisoners. Why not kill someone like Jeb, who in their eyes, was not going to be hurt by his prison experience? In their world, it made sense to lash out at anyone who represented the society that had put them where they were and denied them the opportunity to do anything but repeat the agony. This was their way of getting back at the more privileged among us for not allowing them to be human—for not loving them enough. To anyone outside the prison culture, it made no sense. But I knew it didn't have to.

I thanked Jim and immediately called Jeb's lawyers. Could they do anything to help? I asked. Could they talk to someone and have Jeb sent to another prison? And where would that be? I wondered, even as I was suggesting it. Suppose it was clear across the country where we wouldn't be able to see him? We really didn't have any choice. Jeb's lawyers promised me they would not let him be sent back to Allenwood—but I wondered whether they would be able to make that promise stick.

The next day I got up early, saw the children off to school, and left the house a little after ten. First I went to a Junior League board meeting and then I met a friend, Anne Bull, for lunch in a restaurant in Bethesda. Anne and I hadn't seen each other for months, so we lingered about two hours, talking.

On my way home, I remembered that some of the children's friends were coming for dinner, so I stopped at a supermarket to pick up some extra milk. It was about three o'clock when I drove up the hill toward our house—and then I saw the cars. There must have been a dozen of them, parked on each side of the street. A crowd of people waited outside our house. They were reporters and photographers. I saw cameras, TV lights, and the inevitable microphones.

Suddenly I saw Louie Evans' car among those lined up at the curb. *Something's happened to Jeb!* That was the first thought that came into my mind, and I felt sick.

I had left the garage door open and as I pulled into the driveway, the crowd broke up and let me through.

Another horrible thought came to me. *The children—had there been an accident?* Did the press really want to record my reaction to something like that? Were they that cruel?

I felt so weak I could hardly push the car door open. And then I saw Peggy Arrowsmith, my nextdoor neighbor, running toward me.

"Gail, don't you know?" she said when she saw the fear on my face.

"Know? Know what?"

"Jeb's been released! Judge Sirica ordered it. He and John Dean and Herbert Kalmbach. Gail, he's coming home!"

"I don't believe it!" I said. It was January 8. And I had felt that Jeb would be released in January. Was it possible?

Gilda Herndon, who had been at the League office when the news came in—just after I left for lunch with Anne Bull—came running out from the house and put her arms around me.

"I don't believe it!" I said, yet I was smiling. Part of me was afraid to wake up and find this was only another dream. That had happened before.

Peggy and Gilda led me into the house. Louie was there, waiting to drive me to Holabird. Jeb's release had been announced at 11 o'clock that morning. He called home immediately, but of course he got no answer. *Everybody* was trying to find me!

Stuart was home. He was very excited but a little bewildered. He had spoken to Jeb on the phone, but he was too young to understand the meaning of Jeb's message. "Tell Mommy to come and get me," Jeb had said.

Our house was alive with happy, busy people. Colleen Evans arrived soon after I did, and immediately took charge of the phone, which was ringing itself off the wall. Friends and relatives from all over the country were calling as they heard the news. One of the kindest callers was Patti Colson. Her husband had not been released, yet she called to tell me how happy she was for all of us.

My other covenant sisters were there, straightening up the house and cooking a celebration dinner. I was glad I hadn't taken the tree down because now we could enjoy it together. Some of the friends who stopped by brought gifts—a helium balloon, a lovely pottery mermaid, good things to eat—and we put them under the tree. It really did look like Christmas.

But poor Jeb had been a free man since 11 o'clock that morning, and he was still waiting for me to come and get him.

We were delayed because I wanted the children to come with me, and Justin, Whitney, and Tracy were not yet home. I called their schools to arrange for them to leave early, and then Louie and I went to pick them up. We missed Tracy, who was already on her way home in her usual car pool. Coming up the street, she reacted to the press crowd just as I had. She thought something bad had happened and didn't want to come home, so she went home with one of her friends in the car pool and began helping the girl deliver newspapers. We found her after driving up one street and down another. When we told her about Jeb, she smiled and then broke into tears. I knew exactly how she felt as I held her close to me.

Whitney and Justin were waiting for us outside St. Albans. They were standing a little apart from each other, as if each one needed to be alone to comprehend the wonderful news they had just heard.

We went back to the house to get Stu—and some yellow ribbon. At the time Jeb went into prison, the song "Tie a Yellow Ribbon 'Round the Old Oak Tree" was popular. It was about a young man just out of prison, on his way to see his girl. If he saw a yellow ribbon tied on the old oak tree outside her house, that meant she was waiting for him. As his bus approached the girl's house, the young man was almost afraid to look—but there was the tree covered with yellow ribbons. We didn't have an oak tree in our yard, but the children and I had planned long ago that we would tie yellow ribbons on the little cherry tree in our front yard when Jeb got out. Luckily I had a roll of yellow ribbon in my gift-wrapping box.

Flashbulbs were going off outside as some photographers tried to take pictures through our living-room window. Colleen suggested I go out and talk to the reporters. "It's not like before," she said. "They're happy for you."

Perhaps she was right, but I dreaded facing them. I associated the press with unhappiness.

"Here, take this with you," Colleen said, handing me a yellow ribbon.

She was right. This time it was different. The reporters and photographers were smiling. Several of the women had tears in their eyes. I tied one bow on the cherry tree, but my hands were shaking—and I wanted to go and get Jeb.

Louie Evans drove the children and me in our car. Tom Stone, assistant minister at National Presbyterian Church, followed in Louie's car.

I was going to Holabird for the last time. It was real. *Thank you, thank you, thank you, Lord.*

Outside the main gate to Holabird there was another crowd of reporters and photographers. This time the guards waved us right through, without asking us for identification. Jeb was outside the safe house and came running toward the car as soon as he saw us. Louie stopped the car so I could get out. We held onto each other, crying and laughing, almost hysterical. The children clung to us and Jeb tried to hold all of us in his arms at once. Skitch was there, watching us, with a sad smile on his face.

The bureaucracy was not finished with us yet. "Colonel Klink" told Jeb to come with him to his office where he read him all the rules and regulations regarding his release. Then he went with Jeb to his room to inspect it for any damages or missing government property. Actually, it was in much better condition than it had been when Jeb moved in. He had painted it three times and we had made it more livable with a bedspread, curtains, and an old rug. We had nailed down the rug, so we left it behind.

Jeb was with "Colonel Klink" for about a half hour. The children and I waited in the small TV room, where some of the inmates were watching the evening news. It felt so strange to see myself arriving at home that afternoon and then tying the ribbon on the cherry tree. How could I be so schmaltzy?

One by one, the inmates said good-bye and wished us luck. And then I realized I wouldn't be seeing them again. I was so happy to know Jeb was coming home that there had been room for nothing else in my mind. Now I felt sad, knowing that these men—our friends—had to stay at Holabird. I cried when I saw Eddie—who had observed Christmas with a picture of a hanging man on his door—passing around a bag of his special candies to our children. He had nothing to celebrate, but he was unselfish enough to share in our happiness.

Finally "Colonel Klink" returned with Jeb—and suddenly he was a different man. He shook hands with each of the children and asked them how they were. He wished Jeb and me a good life, and then he said he would show us out a rear gate so we could avoid the press and get home faster. In all the weeks the children and I had been coming to Holabird, this man had hardly spoken a word to us. But that was when Jeb was a prisoner and therefore not considered a human being. Now he was a man—a free man. Now he had feelings. I don't think I had ever seen the nightmare of prison illustrated more sharply.

Skitch and Louie had loaded our car with Jeb's belongings and we were almost ready to go. *What would happen to Skitch?* I wondered. I held onto his hand and kissed him good-bye.

Herb Kalmbach had already left Holabird. He still wouldn't allow his wife to come for him. Instead he went to the airport with a friend and caught a plane to Los Angeles. John Dean hadn't left yet. He was waiting for a friend who would drive him to the airport. He came down to say goodbye and wish us luck. Then he did something very unusual for him. He kissed me on the cheek. That was the only time I have ever seen him express any emotion, and I was surprised and moved.

"Colonel Klink" led us to the rear gate where there were only about ten reporters waiting. Jeb gave them a short statement and we were on our way. Louie Evans and Tom Stone followed in Louie's car.

An hour later we drove into our street. A lovely sight awaited us. My covenant sisters had set up our outdoor spotlights so that they illuminated the little cherry tree covered with yellow bows against the night sky.

At home, there was a beautiful dinner waiting for us, but we were too excited to eat. The table was set with my best crystal and silver, but we hardly had a chance to sit down. More friends and neighbors kept coming by or calling to tell us how happy they were for us. Our dog barked and jumped up on Jeb when she saw him. For a long time, she wouldn't leave his side and her tail wagged constantly as if, yes, now our home was complete again.

We were up very late that night, and it was so wonderful to realize that we didn't have to say good-bye and go our separate ways. Every now and then we hugged each other because it felt so good to be close. Sometimes we felt as if we would choke because our hearts were so filled with love. Our prayers came so easily. There was no self-consciousness about them, no wondering whether they were acceptable to God. He was right there with us and we could feel his love. It was the most joyous experience I have ever known.

14

FOR A PERSON WHO is sent to prison, the sentence never ends. With Jeb's release we were together again as a family—but we were not the same.

Some of the people who wrote to us kept sending letters all the while Jeb was away. It meant so much to me to know that there were men and women I had never met who were praying for us and thinking about us. We mattered to them. When Jeb came home, some of them sent congratulations and good wishes for our future. Then the letters stopped. I've kept all the letters and recently I was going through them. One of them impressed me at the time, and now I find it was prophetic. It came from a woman whose husband had been in prison. She said she was very happy we were all together again, but that now we faced the hardest time of all.

It took me a long time to understand how she meant that, but she was right. In some ways, the period immediately after Jeb's release was the hardest time for us. It's true we weren't separated—at least not in the sense of geographical distance—but there was still an emotional barrier between us. The cruel but simple fact is that, once a man has been dehumanized, he can't become human again overnight.

That was something our friends didn't understand. In fact, they couldn't because they hadn't been through the experience themselves—and that is the only way to learn. They were happy for us and it was only natural for them to think the whole thing was over. *Let's celebrate and then forget it,* was their attitude. I only wish it could have been that simple.

Jeb had to fit back into our family again, and that meant more than going through the motions. He had to see himself as a husband and a father again, which was difficult for him to do without a job. He hadn't really worked in almost two years, and for a man like Jeb that was a special strain. He never has been patient, and in his eagerness to become a bread-winner again he made some errors in judgment. He signed up for a lecture series and agreed to do a promotional tour for the paperback publishers of his book. He was on several TV interview shows. We should have gone away somewhere, just the two of us, to recover from our exhaustion, but instead we went dashing around the country. We had hardly a moment to ourselves.

We all have changed. Stuart seems to struggle the most to adjust to our new way of life. At night, before prison he used to go to sleep the minute his head hit the pillow, but now he is afraid, especially if Jeb is not home. He thinks terrible un-named things are going to happen, I wonder if this is caused by his visits to Allenwood and Holabird or, perhaps, his experiences with the press. He still clings very tightly to Jeb.

There is a new quietness about Tracy. She was always a social child, but now she spends more time by herself.

Justin and Whit had the advantage of more years of normal family living before Jeb went away, and I think that may have helped them. Justin now has a sense of humor and can poke fun at himself, very much as his father can.

Whitney's concerns are less family-related than they used to be. His prayers at the dinner table reflect a growing awareness of human need throughout the world.

Our children are very mature for their age. Their years as "children" were cut short. It will be a long time before we know whether that is a good or a bad thing. It will depend on how it affects their future lives. I like the way they meet their problems head-on, with no pretending or evasion, with no tears or self-pity. And I only hope their gentle Christian faith continues to grow.

Jeb is a different man. He is more sensitive to our needs, and more appreciative of our strengths. A few days after he came home, it rained, and we had water in our basement—for the first time since he went to prison. He had an appointment that day, but he canceled it to stay home and help me mop up. That was something he never would have done before because it wouldn't have occurred to him that such a thing—so unimportant to him—would be upsetting to me.

In the midst of ugliness, Jeb had discovered a hunger for beauty, and that hunger stayed with him after prison. I noticed that he took the time to enjoy a lovely view. He could look at a bare tree in winter and appreciate its basic symmetry and strength. These were the kind of things we never used to be able to do together, and now we can.

But there are still traces of the terrible rigidity I saw in him when he was in prison, and I know that at times he is struggling to keep his emotions under control. At night, when we went to bed before prison, we always used to hold each other very close. Now Jeb lies very still, on his back, arms at his sides, and I know that is the way he used to lie in bed at night in prison. It was the only way for a man to be safe and on guard against attack.

I am different, too. I don't know whether I have become stronger or simply realized my strength, but I am not the same kind of wife. I want to handle more of our family's responsibilities because now I know I can. I want to share in the decision making, and there has to be some of my input in our goals. If the Holy Spirit has indeed given me the gift of insight, then I want it to be of some use to our family. Now, if I have misgivings about some of the people with whom we deal or some of the actions we may consider, I will not be silent about them.

For several months after Jeb's release, he and I were very

depressed. It was almost as if we were recovering from the death of someone close to us. Actually, that wasn't as far-fetched as it may seem—because the child in both of us had died. We couldn't laugh anymore, except at something ironic. Nothing was funny to us. We saw the disappointment on our friends' faces when we didn't respond to their attempts to cheer us up and we understood when they got tired of trying, but we couldn't seem to do anything but allow the pain to work its way through us.

We were not the same—and we didn't know what we were going to be. We only knew that we were waiting.

After that first desperate attempt to get back into a so-called normal life, Jeb stopped short. He had had several job offers—some of them humiliating, some attractive in terms of material benefits—and he followed them up in his usual efficient way. Finally he had to make a choice, and that's when he realized he didn't want any of them. "It would only be the same old hectic life all over again," he told us. "Too much travel, too many phone calls, too much pressure." He did not want to get caught up again in a world of corner-cutting and unethical behavior.

He could not forget the men he had seen in prison, and he wanted to do something to help other people who were being pushed by an uncaring society in the same direction. But how? How could he begin? And was it possible to earn a living at the same time?

Jeb didn't know, but he decided to wait for the answer to come to him. Even though he had been out of prison only a few weeks, he knew he still couldn't help himself. Only God could point out the right direction for us all.

We never had done anything like that before, and naturally we expected the answer to come quickly. After all, didn't God know how desperate we were? Every Sunday after church services, we went downstairs to get the children and have a cup of coffee with our friends. At first, it had been an uplifting experience, but now we were beginning to wish we could avoid it. We knew everyone was concerned about us, but they had been concerned for such a long time, and they were plain worn out. We could see it in their faces when they asked, "How are you?" They wanted so much for us to be able to say, "We're fine—we've got a job," and still we couldn't. We didn't even know where we were going to be living. Surely God understood how worried we were.

Yes, we expected something dramatic, some unmistakable sign that this—or that—was the way for us to go. And day after day nothing happened. If Jeb was offered a job by a Christian service organization—and there were a few—we couldn't live on the salary, even though we had trimmed our needs to the absolute minimum.

Finally there was a more practical offer, and—something equally important—the kind of work Jeb really wanted to do. Still there was no sense of guidance, no nudge to go one way or the other. While we were waiting to find out whether Jeb would really get the job, we didn't know whether to be happy about it if he did. Was this where God wanted us to go?

I know now that guidance doesn't have to take the form of a finger pointing in a particular direction. Sometimes it comes quite methodically. God simply begins removing one obstacle after another—but first, we have to take a step in faith.

Jeb wanted to work with Young Life. We knew from our own children's experience with Chuck Reinhold, our National Presbyterian Youth Minister, who had been with Young Life for ten years, that their techniques for Christian nurture and loving teen-agers worked. Here, in the early years, love, concern, and faith could have a great impact on a person. Here, perhaps, was a way to prevent the prison experience for some of the kids Young Life reaches through its urban and suburban ministry.

Young Life is a Christian service organization that was founded in 1938 by a Dallas minister named Jim Rayburn who was told by his superiors to go out where the kids were and "get something going." And that's what he did. He developed the basic relationship techniques which are now used throughout the country. His aim was to build a relationship with a teen-ager, to be his friend. Then, when a relationship of love and trust existed, the teen-ager was ready to hear about Jesus Christ.

Today, through its camps and hundreds of specially trained counselors, Young Life is reaching out to teen-agers in cities, suburbs, and small towns. These young people are at that age where they are questioning and doubting so much about life, other people, and themselves. The Young Life counselors aim to help them develop the kind of trusting relationships that will lead them to accept Jesus Christ as their Savior. In Young Life summer camps, young men and women learn rock climbing, backpacking, swimming, and stress camping, and in so doing they learn to appreciate the strength of their bodies. Most of them come away with a sense of self-worth that can change the direction of their lives.

The men Jeb had seen in prison might have been Young Life kids if they had had the chance. That was one of the reasons the organization appealed to him. It offered him a chance to live productively and help guide others toward a more meaningful life.

Young Life had made Jeb an offer, and after several interviews they made it firm. Now it was up to us.

So many things about the job were good. We needed to get away from Washington, and Young Life headquarters are in Colorado Springs. Jeb would have a chance to contribute his administrative abilities, which have always been excellent. We would be nurtured in our Christian faith by our close association with Young Life workers—and we needed that.

Jeb would have to prepare himself for a different kind of

world. He likes to get things done quickly, and, in that sense, he enjoys the fast pace of the business world. But a Christian organization moves more slowly. It does not go for the jugular. Instead, its members try to work out their misunderstandings patiently because they are motivated more by fellowship than competition. Whatever their differences, they are united by their common goal of service in the name—and love—of the Lord.

But there were problems, too. We didn't know what kind of schools were available for our children—and here it was June, with school opening in eight weeks. We didn't know whether we could find a house quickly, and for the right amount of money.

We decided we would just have to begin moving in the direction that seemed right for us, and trust God to let us know if we were wrong. Jeb accepted the job and we took a short trip to Colorado Springs. We brought Whitney along so that he could see the new area and, hopefully, transmit his excitement to our younger children.

And then the obstacles began to be removed. The school Whit liked best was right in the heart of the city, which surprised us, because we always had lived in the suburbs. But our son had had a broad experience of people and he liked the prospect of going to school with children from many different backgrounds. When he saw the catalogue of courses—almost an inch thick—he was thrilled. He never had had such a choice.

The school determined where we wanted to live, but in the neighborhood we selected there were no houses for sale. It was an old, established, tree-shaded part of the city where very few families moved in and out. Our real estate agent said she thought one young couple might be thinking of moving to the mountains—where she had a piece of property they might like—but she didn't want to get our hopes up.

It was amazing. The house was exactly what we wanted

—three stories high, with lots of large rooms, and very old—
and the young couple said yes, they would be willing to sell it,
because they had been thinking of moving to the mountains.
And again, yes, the transaction could be completed in time for
our children to begin school on August 25. Jeb and I just
looked at each other, and I think we smiled from the inside
out for the first time in years.

At last, our depression began to lift. Jeb knew where he
was going to work and I knew where we were going to live. I
had never realized how important these two things were. We
felt as if we had just sprouted two roots in new soil, and we
knew now that our plant was going to live.

As we made our preparations to move and begin our
new life, there were many things on my mind. I didn't understand all that had happened to us, and I doubt I ever will.
I still feel some bitterness because I know that many people
who were involved in Watergate have gone unpunished. Some
of them have important jobs and are making a lot of money—
and some of them are going through hell. I don't envy them,
and I don't like feeling bitter about them, either. These are
feelings I have to work out of my system, with God's help.

I know that there were many people in the past who
committed similar crimes and broke as many laws, and they
too have gone unpunished. I also know that of all the persons
who commit crimes of any kind, most are not apprehended.
Of those who are arrested, only a relative few are sentenced to
prison. To me, that doesn't seem fair.

I think that sometimes God has to bring a nation up
short and make an example of some of its people, and perhaps
this is what he did through Watergate. I think it has had its
effect on the behavior of men in government—and that is
good.

I agree with Jeb about Richard Nixon. I believe it is just
as well that he was pardoned. I say this because I know something about what our judicial system and prison do to a person

and his family—and it doesn't do anything good. I wish we could come up with a better way of dealing with those who break laws and commit crimes. I know we can't ignore crime, because society also must be protected from violence and deceit, but what we are doing is not right.

I won't forget the men I met at Allenwood and Holabird. We still keep in touch with Skitch, who was sent to a prison in the Southwest after Holabird was closed down. He is too far away for his wife and child to visit him, so that is one more family virtually destroyed by the prison system. Skitch has several more years to serve before he becomes eligible for parole, and sometimes, he doesn't seem to care about getting out. But there are other signs—little signs—that tell us something else is going on inside him. He is taking a course in air-conditioning repair, and for Skitch that expresses a remarkable optimism. And at Christmas we received a card from him—with a nativity scene on the cover.

I worry about Skitch's wife and their little boy. They are innocent victims of the bureaucracy and bigness of our society. They react to hurt and violence. If that child is not reached with a tremendous amount of love, he will grow into a violent adult. I am certain of that. I also am certain that the only one who can love him enough is Jesus Christ. The problem is, how do we get Jesus Christ close enough to touch him? That is something for all of us to ponder.

I often think about Bill, and Sal, and Dave, and Angelo, and Paulo, and Gino, and Leo, and Eddie. I owe them so much. Never again will I think of a person as a member of a group—and therefore condemn him. Each one is a person, made in the image of God. Each is a child of God, just as I am. These men are my brothers. And my brothers are hurting.

Dear Lord, what can I do to help them?

Epilogue

THERE ARE SOME THINGS I wish for my family:

I hope we can be close together in the few years that are left before our children go off to build lives of their own. I hope we can do it quietly, away from the public spotlight.

I hope our children will not be scarred by the traumatic events in the lives of their parents.

I hope my husband and I can do productive, creative work that will be of value to others.

I pray that my children, my husband, and I will continue to grow in the Lord.